101 WAYS TO PUT PIZAZZ INTO YOUR TEACHING

Bonnie Williamson

Dynamic Teaching Company
Post Office Box 276711
Sacramento, CA 95827

101 WAYS TO PUT PIZAZZ INTO YOUR TEACHING
By Bonnie Williamson

Published by: Dynamic Teaching Company
                Post Office Box 276711
                Sacramento, CA 95827
                Telephone: (916) 351-1912
                Fax Orders: (916) 985-7832

First printing 1991

Printed in the United States of America

Cover and Book Design by Robert Howard Graphic Design

Editor: Marilyn Pribus

Illustrations: Sandy Thornton

Typesetting: Pauline Howard

Library of Congress cataloging in Publication Data

Williamson, Bonnie
        101 Ways To Put Pizazz Into Your Teaching
        Includes resources
1. Classroom ideas
2. Education, Elementary
3. Student teacher resources
4. Classroom management
5. Teachers, Classroom
I. Title

Library of Congress Catalog Number 91-070644

ISBN 0-937899-12-7

To my friend and editor Lynn Pribus, who has done an outstanding job editing all of my books while at the same time encouraging me each step of the way, I give my most sincere appreciation.

My sincere thanks to Sandra Oi for her contributions to the chapter on music in the classroom.

My thanks also to Sandy Thornton, Kathy Hoff, Robert and Pauline Howard — the rest of the book team.

OTHER BOOKS BY BONNIE WILLIAMSON

A First-Year Teacher's Guidebook for Success
Classroom Management: A Guidebook for Success
Parent Power: A Guide to Your Child's Success

TABLE OF CONTENTS

Dear Teacher,

During my twenty-seven years as a teacher, I frequently taught when we had a shortage of textbooks, no resource teachers and no enrichment materials. One September I even had to race out the night before school started to buy thirty-four pencils for my students.

It was during these cost-cutting periods that I began to develop my own enrichment materials. Many of these lessons you'll find in this book. My students enjoyed the "extra pizazz" these lessons brought into the "dailyness" of school as I did.

Other ideas came from master teachers who shared their ideas at workshops. I am indeed grateful to them for enriching my "cache of pizazz lessons."

To you, the teachers of the 90s and beyond, my hope is that you too will see smiles on your students' faces as you use the ideas found in this book.

Bonnie Williamson
Sacramento, CA
1991

Chapter 1

Reading and Language Ideas

- Making Your Students into Recording Stars
- Writing a Story About a Building
- Animal Story
- Choral Reading
- Poetry in Motion
- Nursery Rhymes
- Puppets in the Classroom

Reading and Language Ideas

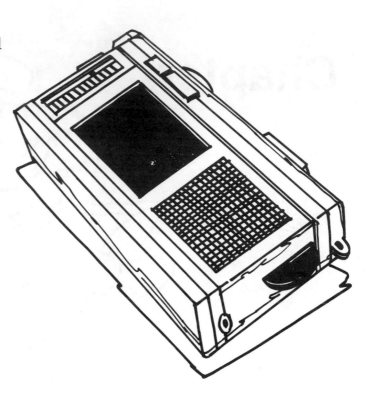

Objectives
- To encourage students to become good readers
- To help children feel comfortable telling stories
- To teach the joy of poetry

Materials
Cassette player and tape
Plastic sandwich bags
Paper for pictures and names
Mailers for cassette tapes
Postage stamps
Hand and finger puppets
Two baskets

Suggested Ages
Seven to twelve

Lesson

MAKING YOUR STUDENTS INTO RECORDING STARS

Primary Students: Do this reading activity with one group at a time and alternate week by week. Assign a story Monday and continue to do all reading skills until Thursday. Tell the group that they will be making a cassette tape on Friday. (The other group will do quiet activities while taping is going on.)

On Friday have each student decide which page of the story he or she wants to read and choose a person to read to. Some students, for example, might wish to nominate a relative or friend who is ill, a grandparent or younger sibling.

Give each child two slips of paper to put into two baskets, one for the page and one for the name. Note that Glenn's slips say he wants to read page 62 to his sister. Also, explain to the students that if their page has already been drawn from the basket, they must be prepared with a second choice.

First the teacher draws one slip from the "Reading-for-Friends" basket. The "winner" will receive the tape with several different students reading. The student who nominated the winner will automatically be the first reader.

Next draw slips from the "Read-Aloud" basket and list the students' names and pages in sequential order.

Here is an example of how the chalkboard would look:

NAME	PAGE
Glenn	p. 62
Joaquin	p. 63
Tina	p. 64

• *We are reading today for Jennifer, Glenn's sister.*

Before beginning to read, instruct the students to read slowly and speak clearly when it is their turn to read into the tape recorder.

Remind them it is their responsibility to look at the board and be ready to read when the current reader begins the final sentence on their page.

EXAMPLE OF AN INTRODUCTION

"Good morning, Jennifer. I'm Glenn's teacher, Mrs. Williamson. This is my *Full Circle* reading group. We will be reading the story 'Picasso.' Please open Glenn's book to page 62 and follow along."

Glenn says, "Hello, Jennifer, this is Glenn and I'll be reading page 62. Joaquin and Tina will follow me." At the end of the story, the teacher will thank the child for listening and say, "Maybe you would like to draw your own picture of the story for Glenn to share with the class tomorrow."

Naturally your students will want to hear the tape. While they listen, pass out small pieces of art paper (about 4" x 6") and have students illustrate the story. Ask one child to make the cover with the story title and Jennifer's name on the front. Staple the booklet together and place it with the tape in a small plastic bag to send home with Glenn. Remind him you'd like the tape or a replacement back within three days for recycling.

Reading and Language Ideas

If you make a tape for someone outside your school community, you will need inexpensive mailers which require two stamps. You'll have to decide if you'll supply the mailers and stamps.

I have found this tape lesson is extremely popular with my parents, younger siblings and relatives. Give it a try!

Intermediate Students: In the upper grades, you could form a committee of students who would, in turn, elect a leader. This person could serve to introduce the story and those taking part. If you provide them with blank tapes, they can record stories to be placed in the classroom tape library. Then when students finish their lessons, they can go to the tape library and using a headset, listen to a story.

WRITING A STORY ABOUT A BUILDING — A LANGUAGE LESSON

Children are much more motivated to write when they can identify with the subject. Have your students write about a building near the school. This might be the bus shed, a fire station, library or unusual home.

Prior to writing, talk about the building. On the chalkboard or overhead list the various characteristics of the building such as: tall, looks like a box, has many windows.

In another column list words which describe what might be inside. If you've chosen a firehouse, include words like: fire engine, firemen, ladders, or hoses.

In another column, write words which describe the people and animals that might be inside. Five firefighters, one dog, two cats, one bird, even a baby elephant. Stretch your childrens' imaginations!

Talk about "describing words" and "action words." List some of these.

Help the students begin a rough draft of the story, then have them continue to develop their own stories. Each day allow time to review and edit the story for punctuation, spelling, and grammar. This review may be done with a partner. As a final step, have them draw pictures to illustrate the story.

After the final drafts are written, take the class on a walking field trip to the building to check out their accuracy. If you wrote about a fire station, for example, arrange ahead of time for them to meet the firefighters and even give them some of the stories. As you walk around the building and go inside, see if there are animals.

ANIMAL STORY — A LANGUAGE LESSON

Animals are often part of the classroom environment. Take advantage of this by having children write about the classroom rabbit, fish, guinea pig, rat or hamster. Some rooms even have a cat as a pet.

Before beginning, talk about a title and remind students to indent their paragraphs and use proper endings for all sentences. Later have your students illustrate their stories and read them aloud in class.

TIMELY TIP: **Some newspapers are interested in publishing stories about unusual things going on in classrooms. If you have an interesting pet in your classroom, have your students write a story. Taking a photo of the pet and sending it along may help get it published. Call your newspaper to see if they would be interested. Students love to see their names in print.**

For additional information on writing tips, see Teacher Resources on page 132.

CHORAL READING

If you have reluctant readers, try choral reading. Students enjoy reading as a group and you'll find it easier to keep them on task. The first time you do this start with a short poem. Gradually work up to fifteen minutes or so with an entire story. Demonstrate the pace you wish to use. Remind students that when saying the Pledge of Allegiance, for example, we speak slowly so all can take part. The same is true in choral reading.

Be sure all students are on the correct page in the reader, count to three and then all begin. At the end of each page, have all students stop, take a deep breath and wait till you count to three before beginning the next page.

Reading and Language Ideas

POETRY IN MOTION

- Use poetry to illustrate the rhythm of language.
- Poetry in the classroom helps to build pictures in your students' minds.
- Poetry is one way for your students to express their emotions and feelings.

Each month have your class memorize one poem. It can relate to a holiday, a subject you are studying or come from their reading book.

As an added incentive, suggest your students bring props to dramatize the poem. Tell them they can earn points or a higher grade depending upon the number of props they bring.

Halloween, for example, is a delightful time of year for poems. Model an example for your students. Turn off the lights, sit on a stool and wear a tall black witch hat, a long black dress and vocalize in your "witch-type" voice.

The students will love this. Consider also assigning poems for Thanksgiving, Christmas, Valentine's Day and Easter.

See page 132 in Teacher Resources for art ideas to go along with holidays.

TIMELY TIP: **It is helpful if you appoint one student as a prop person to work in the back of the room to help students get ready to "go on stage." This keeps the action going and illustrates to your students how to put on a poem presentation for the class.**

NURSERY RHYMES

Primary students, in particular, enjoy hearing and saying nursery rhymes. Select eight or ten of their favorites and place these on 3" x 5" cards. Keep in a file near your desk.

When you have a couple of minutes before the recess bell rings, say the rhyme to your class. Do this several times in a dramatic voice. As soon as you feel the majority of students know the lines, ask them to say it as a group.

TIMELY TIP: **Use nursery rhymes as sponges (fillers for available minutes) while your class is standing in line. This can be while waiting to go outside for recess, lunch or to go home. Their energy level is high at this time and you'll find them most enthusiastic about these group recitations.**

USING PUPPETS IN THE CLASSROOM

Children are delighted when a puppet show comes to the school. However, instead of paying for a group, you can put on your own show. Use a refrigerator box with the upper portion of one side cut out for the "stage" or drape a sheet over several desks and have the students operate the puppets behind the desks.

Most reading books have simple plays which you can use with puppets or you may wish to purchase a book on puppeteering at a teacher store. Sometimes a book will have patterns drawn so the students can make the puppets themselves.

TIMELY TIP: **If you wish to have a puppeteer or a ventriloquist come to your classroom, call your local Parks and Recreation Department for suggestions or look in the yellow pages of the phone book under "Talent Agencies."**

Reading and Language Ideas

FINGER PUPPETS

Primary students, in particular, enjoy finger puppets. You can buy them at novelty stores or through a teacher store catalog.

For example, *The Tale of Peter Rabbit* comes alive when told by finger puppets representing Flopsy, Mopsy, Cottontail and Peter.

Also, some parents are most clever at making puppets. Ask them. Remember, "Puppets make stories come to life."

TIMELY TIP: **Keep in mind that your students will listen more carefully to a story told by a puppet than one told by you. When telling a story through a puppet, be sure to dramatize it through exaggerated mannerisms and varied "voices" for your characters. Your students will ask for more!**

Chapter 2

Making Math Count

- Toss Out

- King Math

- Chanting Math Facts

- Rope Math

- Multiplication Trains

- Place Value

Making Math Count

Objective
• To teach basic math facts

Materials
Hole punch
3" x 5" cards
Overhead projector

Suggested Ages
Six to twelve

Lesson

MATH DOMINOS

Here is a simple game to teach your class basic math facts. Cut 3" x 5" cards into 1 1/2" squares. Use a hole punch to make two sets of cards from one to nine. In upper grades go to twelve. See sample.

Pass out paper. Have students place their names on top and number from 1 to 10. Explain you'll put two dominos on the overhead and turn it on for only five seconds. During that time and a few seconds afterward, they must record the fact and write down the answer.

In the primary grades, using an overhead projector pen, draw a **+** or **-** between two dominos and an **=** sign at the end. In the intermediate grades use a **x** sign as well. This is a five-minute activity to use after returning from recess or at the end of a math period.

Objective
• To teach place value

Materials
Several decks of playing cards
One playing sheet for each student (as illustrated)

Suggested Ages
Six to twelve

Lesson

TOSS OUT

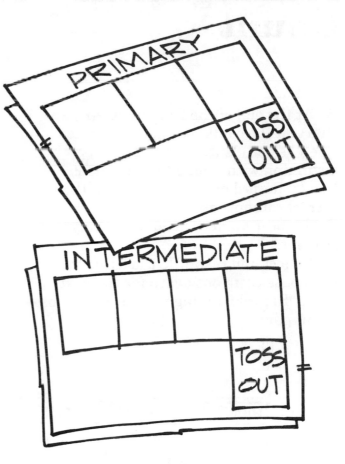

This popular activity teaches place value.

Make a ditto like the sample shown for primary grades. For intermediate students, add thousands as shown. The spaces should be the size of the playing cards you are using.

Take several decks of playing cards and remove the face cards and tens. Explain to primary students that they will each be given four cards ranging from Ace (equals 1) to nine. Intermediate students will need five cards each.

Tell your students they must not look at the cards and must keep them face down on the corner of their desks all during the game. They may not lift the top card until the teacher gives a signal. Explain the object of the game is to get the highest score. In primary grades, this would be 999. In the upper grades it would be 9,999.

At a snap of your fingers, they are to pick up the top card and decide where to place it. The first few times you play, give them ten seconds to decide, but decrease the time as you play. You'll continue to pause, then snap your fingers until all spaces are filled. Explain that the best chance of winning comes from placing highest cards in the hundreds space for primary and in the thousand space for intermediates and, if possible, a 9 card in all other spaces except the Toss-Out space. Alert your students that if they bring up an Ace or any low number, it should be placed in the Toss-Out space because the Toss-Out space doesn't count.

SUGGESTIONS: Remind your students that once a card is placed on the playing board (number side up) they cannot move the card.

Making Math Count

At the end of the first game, draw a chart on the chalkboard as illustrated. Then ask students having a number beginning with a nine to raise their hands. Record all the numbers in the correct columns and draw a big star by the highest number attained by any student.

Collect and reshuffle the cards and then pass them out again for the next game. Record winning numbers for subsequent games.

Objectives
• To teach primary students addition and subtraction facts
• To teach intermediate students multiplication facts

Material
One jumbo-size deck of playing cards

Suggested Ages
Six to twelve

Lesson

KING MATH

This is a game enjoyed by both primary and intermediate students. For best results play in groups of four. Usually one group at a time will play.

Purchase a package of giant playing cards. Shuffle the cards and explain to your students that the Kings, Queens and Jacks will all have a value of 10. The Ace equals one.

Use the cards to teach addition facts and multiplication facts to intermediates.

Place the deck of cards face down and toss a die to determine who starts. The winner takes two cards off the deck. If the student drew an eight and seven, for example, the correct response would be 8 + 7 = 15. The next student draws and the game continues until all cards have been drawn. In intermediate grades the students would say 8 x 7 = 56, etc. Everyone is a winner because they are learning their basic math facts.

Objective

- To teach the basic facts

Suggested Ages

Ages six to twelve

Lesson

CHANTING MATH FACTS

In the primary grades, students must know their addition and subtraction facts. By intermediate grades, they also need to know their multiplication facts. One way to help them do this is by chanting the facts as a group for four or five minutes at a time.

For example if you wanted them to know that 3 + 5 = 8 you would stand in front of the room and count to three. Then clap your hands as you chant, *"Three plus five equals eight."* When you come to the word *"equals"* push your elbows backward, then clap again while saying *"eight."*

In the intermediate grades you might wish to have your students snap fingers instead of clapping the multiplication facts. *Say: "Three times four equals twelve." Snap: X X Pause (bend elbows back) X.*

Quickly and quietly count 1-2-3 and repeat the fact. Do three times (or longer if some students don't know it yet).

A more advanced fact to chant would be: *Say: "Eight times six equals forty-eight." Clap: X Pause X (bend elbows back) XX (clap twice).*

TIMELY TIP: **Did you know that students must see, say or write a math fact, spelling word or vocabulary word twenty-six times before it is imprinted in their minds? Always keep this in mind as you prepare your lessons. Think of as many ways as you can to get math facts across (correctly) twenty-six times.**

Making Math Count

Objectives
• To teach primary students addition facts
• To teach intermediate students multiplication facts

Materials
Cotton ropes about 1/2" thick
Three 40" long ropes for every two students in class
Plastic tape to cover cut ends of rope

Lesson

ROPE MATH

Purchase enough rope to make three 40" ropes for each pair of students in your classroom. You should be able to do this for about $10, depending upon the size of your class. Cut the ropes into 40" lengths and seal ends with plastic tape.

TIMELY TIP: **Place ropes in a box, label "Rope Math" and keep it away from all Physical Education equipment. Otherwise, students will grab them at recess time and try to use them as jump ropes. Have your students use them only under your supervision as part of math lessons.**

Before taking your students outside, tell them exactly what you want them to do. Explain that you want them to work in pairs and each pair will have three ropes. See page 132 in Teacher Resources for diagram.

SUGGESTIONS: Do not let students just race outside without telling them where to stand. Explain that you'll be using three sides of the kickball field, for example, which has lines drawn.

Tell your students that five pairs will stand on the right side of the kickball court, five pairs at the top and five pairs on the left side. Draw this on your chalkboard so they will understand before going out. Explain that a student without a partner may join a pair.

Designate one student to take the Rope Math box outside and place it in the middle of the kickball court. One student of each pair will take three ropes out of the box for that pair to use. The ropes are to be laid out as illustrated.

Explain you'll snap your fingers and call out one math fact such as: 9 + 7 = ___. Each pair will then use the ropes to form the answer, 16, on the ground. As soon as the number is formed, they are to stand and wait quietly.

After all answers have been formed, have everyone clap the complete fact. (See Chanting math facts, page 13.)

This is done by the teacher counting to three and then all together the group says, "Nine plus seven equals sixteen."

Intermediates: Use the same method for multiplication facts.

HINT: At end of each lesson, have one student from each pair place their ropes in "Rope Box," and designate one student to take the box back into classroom.

Objective

• To help students memorize multiplication facts

Materials

Small items such as buttons, beans or acorns
(Allow at least 56 for each student)
Containers

Suggested Ages

Nine to twelve

Lesson

MULTIPLICATION TRAINS

Here's a "hands-on" approach to teach both the understanding and memorization of the multiplication facts.

1. Model on the overhead projector what you wish the students to do. Use small movable objects such as buttons, beans or acorns.

Write on the top of the overhead a multiplication fact such as: 7 x 4 = 28.

Arrange 28 beans in a single row as shown here:

Then say, "Now watch how I'm going to arrange this train into seven individual sets." Do the separating with your finger while the students watch the screen.

It will look like this:

•••• •••• •••• •••• •••• •••• ••••

Ask, "How many sets do we have?"
"How many beans in each set?"
"How many beans all together?"

Ask the students to clap the multiplication fact, "7 x 4 = 28." (See page 13 for instruction on clapping.)

TIMELY TIP: **Plan ahead. Obtain enough small, durable containers so each student will have one. Take either a tray or lid of a box and arrange the cups in the lid. Place at least 56 beans in each cup. You need not count except for first cup. Note height of beans in cup and use this as a guide for filling the rest.**

Making Math Count

Objective
• To help young students understand place value

Materials
Beans, small paper cups and plastic strawberry baskets

Suggested Ages
Five to seven

Lesson

PLACE VALUE

Here is a simple idea which works well to teach place value in the primary grades. Collect plastic strawberry baskets until you have enough to count out rectangles with ten little openings. Be sure each child has one frame as illustrated.

Place a small paper cup holding twenty beans on each desk. Ask your students to put a bean in each square. When finished, explain that they've just made one 10. Then ask them to put two loose beans beside the frame and explain they've just made the number "12." Play for about five minutes each day at the opening of the math lesson for at least three weeks. Review a month later to be sure all students have retained the information.

TIMELY TIP: **Before beginning this activity, remind your students that the beans must be used at their desk only. They are not to be thrown or poked into their noses, mouths or ears. One boy who put a bean into his ear developed earaches. By the time the doctor dug it out, it had sprouted. Remind your students this is not the place to grow beans!**

Ideas
For more good math ideas to use in your classroom, see page 132 in Teacher Resources.

Chapter 3

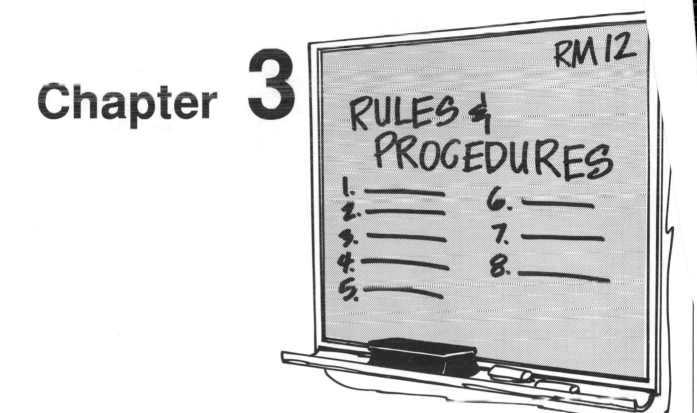

Classroom Management

- Desk Arrangements
- Quiet Zone
- Bags: Parts I and II
- Monitoring Students
- Marking Time

Classroom Management

Objectives
• To arrange your classroom effectively
• To keep your room quiet and minimize disruptive behavior

Materials
Desks
Rug
Bags, large and small, paper and plastic
Timer
Empty can
Spray paint
Fire-retardant spray (maybe)

Suggested Ages
Six to twelve

DESK ARRANGEMENTS

During the opening month of school arrange your students' desks in traditional rows. This gives you good eye contact while teaching procedures and rules. The formal classroom arrangement dictates that students face forward and listen.

After several weeks, try some different configurations. Whether you use the Cooperative Learning desk arrangement (see illustration) or other set-ups, be sure to allow plenty of space between desks so you can reach each student easily. Also, be sure you can view all students and they can see you. This will cut down on behavior problems.

TIMELY TIP: **Some students may stay only a short time before moving on. In order to help you maintain a peaceful transition for new students coming into your room, prepare for them ahead of time. Obtain an extra desk and place it in a row or station. Equip the desk with pencil, paper, books and scissors so when the new student arrives, you'll have a desk all ready. This is a very welcoming gesture to a new student and lessens disruption for you. While the desk is not being used, use it as a barrier between misbehaving students.**

QUIET ZONE

Unless you teach in a new school, you probably do not have a rug. If you don't, consider buying one. Check discount rug centers or even garage sales for good buys.

Ask your principal if you must have the rug sprayed with fire retardant. Once your rug is installed, you'll notice a wonderful change in the classroom atmosphere; quiet will prevail.

If your custodian is not available to vacuum your rug, purchase an inexpensive electric sweeper, perhaps at a used furniture store. Let students take turns vacuuming as one of the jobs in your classroom. They love doing this and it teaches responsibility at the same time it helps you.

BAGS: PART I (BIG)

Always keep plenty of large brown grocery bags on hand. They come in very handy when a student's backpack splits, after class parties or projects when children are loaded down with things to take home and at the end of the year. If you require that your students clean their desks each Friday, the bags are helpful for getting papers home.

BAGS: PART II (SMALL)

Small plastic or paper bags are very handy in the classroom too. Use them to send home a tooth which came out in class, uneaten snacks or a few crayons for a child who has none at home and needs to finish a project.

MONITORING STUDENTS

You need to know where your students are at all times. One way to monitor them is to attach a Hall Pass board to the wall next to the classroom door. Teacher stores feature colorful boards with pegs and hanging passes for students to use, or you could devise your own. Be sure your students carry the passes when going to the nurse, restroom, office and library.

Classroom Management

MARKING TIME

One of the handiest items you can have on your desk is a timer. Set it to go off five minutes before recess or lunch period so you can have your class ready to leave without rushing. This will lead to a quieter dismissal and fewer frayed nerves for you. Use it to time tests or small-group activities. You can also use it as a reminder for particular students to go to the nurse, speech teacher or resource teacher.

TIMELY TIP: **If your students are not sure where to line up when the bell rings or where to go during a fire drill, mark the spot for them. Cut out both ends of an empty 16-oz. can and rinse well. Purchase some bright red exterior spray paint and use the can as a guide to paint a red circle where you wish your students to line up. Make another circle where your students line up when you go outside for a fire drill. This will eliminate confusion.**

For more detailed information on classroom management, see page 132 in Teacher Resources.

Chapter 4

Bulletin Board Magic

- Room Atmosphere
- Bulletin Boards
- Murals
- A Timeline

Bulletin Board Magic

Objectives
• To provide students with the opportunity to decorate their classroom
• To introduce a variety of art mediums to students
• To teach the sequence of history

Materials
Fabric
Newsprint, roll ends
Crayons
Wire
Magic Markers

Suggested Ages
Six to twelve

Lesson

ROOM ATMOSPHERE

Students enjoy being in a light, bright, colorful classroom. Do as much as you can to provide an enjoyable place for them — and for you — to work each day.

BULLETIN BOARDS

Bulletin boards are an important part of your classroom, not just for decoration, but also as a teaching tool to illustrate and enhance the units you are teaching.

TIMELY TIP: A recent study indicates a correlation between certain colors being used in the classroom and the amount of nervous energy exhibited by students. The study states that bright yellows and oranges can create behavior problems for children. On the other hand, the cool colors such as blues and greens have a calming effect. Consider this when you do your bulletin boards.

Bulletin boards don't always need to be arranged from construction paper. One teacher, for example, discovered a bright cotton fabric designed with rulers drawn all over it. She used this to cover one large bulletin board to introduce the new math series to her students in September.

The border was formed by using large pieces of black rick rack. She even had enough fabric left to make a matching "math dress" to wear the opening day of school.

MURALS

Each month mount a long piece of paper on one wall at student height to provide students with the opportunity to create their own pictures. Decide on a topic for the monthly mural and then set the rules. For example, work must be finished and only four students at the mural at a time. Students waiting can put their names on the chalkboard and take turns with those working at the mural.

In the primary grades, it is important for the teacher to print the title of the picture at the top of the mural and draw in the horizon line. Students should use crayons.

In the intermediate grades, a brief discussion by the teacher on the theme and what is needed is usually sufficient. Intermediates enjoy using magic markers and colored pencils to complete their mural.

TIMELY TIP: **Always be on the lookout for items you can use on bulletin boards. Watch for fabrics on bargain tables, artificial flowers, toys, souvenirs, books, magazines, costume jewelry, games, posters, baskets and other items that spark the imagination. Check out flea markets, thrift stores and garage sales.**

WIRE LINE

An interesting variation on bulletin boards is a wire line. Check with your principal about putting up a wire from one end of your room to the other. If it's not allowed, use small hooks and run the line from hook to hook. You may need to get the custodian to help you do this. Purchase colorful plastic clothes pins to display outstanding artwork, timely posters and craft projects including embroidery.

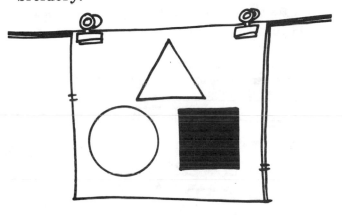

TIMELY TIP: **A good way to get inexpensive, large roll ends of wide paper is at your local newspaper office. Many of them will sell you rolls of newsprint at a most-reasonable price.**

Bulletin Board Magic

A TIMELINE

You can also use the wire as a timeline when teaching history. For example, have a committee of students work on important dates in the history of your state.

Have the students draw an outline of the state on construction paper and cut out many. Have them note the date the state was discovered, date the first capitol building was built, and dates of other important events and hang the cutouts in sequence. This gives students a sense of order as they move from date to date and helps them retain the sequence of history.

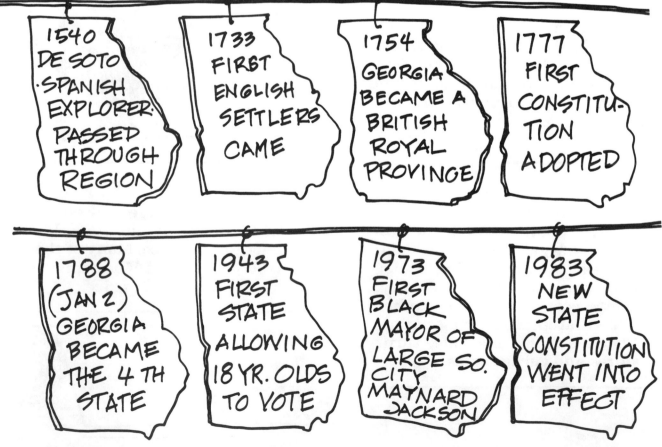

Chapter 5

Lesson Plans
and Seating Charts

- Quick Seating Charts
- Seating Success

Lesson Plans and Seating Charts

Objectives
• To provide ideas to help with writing lesson plans
• To present a simple way to keep a seating chart

Materials
Stick 'um notes
Colored pens
Paper
Manila folder
Lesson Plan Book

Lesson

Lesson plans are vital each day, not only for you but for a substitute in case you must be absent. Arrange a specific time each week when you sit down and do your plans. This will relieve your mind so you can get on with your teaching.

To make your plans more interesting, use colored pens to color code academic subjects, recess, lunch periods, yard duty and field trips. Draw pictures to illustrate TV, video and film showings.

Be good to yourself. Always use a bright pen when writing your plans and on the Monday square write, "Welcome Back! Have a great week!" Then draw a smiling face. You'll be surprised on Monday mornings how this warm greeting will help you begin your week with a smile.

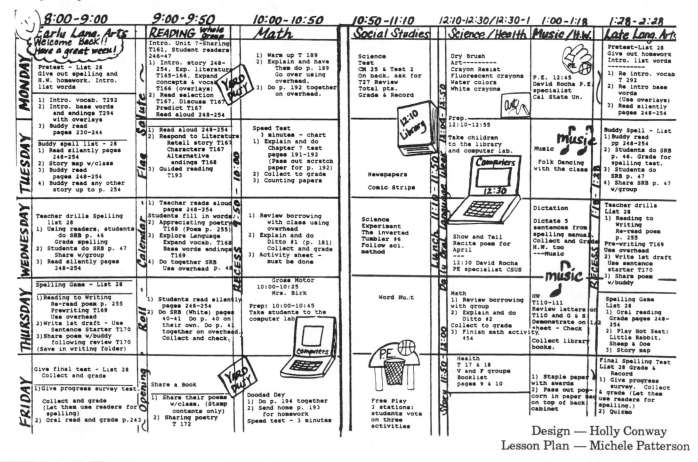

Design — Holly Conway
Lesson Plan — Michele Patterson

TIMELY TIP: **Always leave complete lesson plans in case you might be absent. Substitutes are most unhappy to find no lesson plans and have been known to complain to the principal. At evaluation time, this can come back to haunt you. Be prepared and then you can relax, knowing your class will be well taken care of while you're away.**

If you have access to a computer, obtain software disks which are available for writing lesson plans, recording grades and providing you with a teacher's calculator. For more information see page 132 in the Teacher Resources.

TIMELY TIP: **If you're at ease with a typewriter, you might wish to use it to do your lesson plans. Cut the pages for each week out of your Lesson Plan Book and type the lessons. If using a computer, custom tailor a plan page. When finished, return them to the Lesson Plan Book and attach with a large paper clip.**

QUICK SEATING CHARTS

Before school begins, decide upon one or two seating arrangements to use in your room during the year. Draw these on 8 1/2" x 11" paper and make several photocopies to save in a folder. Then purchase 2" x 1 1/2" stick 'um pads and cut them in half lengthwise.

Write each student's name on a stick 'um and place the slip on the desk you've drawn on the paper. If a problem develops, move them around! Also, as students move in and out, you can discard or add as needed.

TIMELY TIP: **Substitute teachers get very upset when seating charts are not up-to-date. In some classrooms, mischievous students will change seats, creating problems when the sub calls out the wrong name. Be sure your chart is updated weekly, especially when you will not be in school. Subs appreciate this.**

Lesson Plans and Seating Charts

SEATING SUCCESS

You'll never find the perfect seating arrangement in your classroom because as soon as you do, a student will move away, upsetting your great plans. However, here is a clue which can help. Use the shapes illustrated here as model desks. After a month in school, you should know your students well. Take your class list and this "A-B-C" code to assign letters to your students:

A = active
B = behavior
C = content

On each desk write a name and place either an "A" or "B" or "C" after the name.

For example: Tony loves to talk and talk. He will talk to anyone around him. He is not a behavior problem but a talker. He would be considered an "A".

Corey is a Behavior problem with a capital "B". He hits other students, calls them horrible names and is always in trouble. Put a "B" after his name.

Anita is so quiet you'd hardly know she is in your room. She is also a pleaser. She wants to help you clean off the bookshelf, tidy up the drainboard and help Stacy with her math. She is content. Put a "C" after her name.

Once you have all your students lettered, pick up your seating chart and rearrange your students using the "A-B-C" letter code to guide you. You would never, of course, put three "B" students together. Instead, put them far from each other and, if possible, on the corner of a station, end of a row or with an empty desk between them and the next student.

Carefully thinking through how you arrange your three types of students will certainly help your classroom management system.

For a sample of the shapes, turn to page 132 in Teacher Resources.

SAMPLE DESK ARRANGEMENT

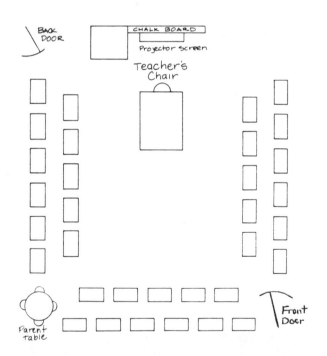

Directions:

1. Arrange your "B" students first using either stick 'um pads or the cut outs on page 132 in Teacher Resources.
2. Mix "A" and "C" students to provide proper balance for your "B" students.

Chapter 6

Seasonal Art

- Stained Glass Windows
- Tissue Pumpkins
- A Christmas Ornament
- A Christmas Plate
- A Blooming Tree for Spring

Seasonal Art

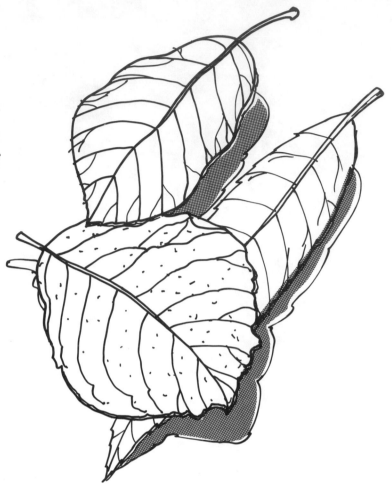

Objectives
- To teach students to follow directions
- To practice using several materials to construct a picture
- To help students experience the joy of making things and sharing ideas

Materials
Construction paper
Waxed paper
Crayons
Iron
Towels
Grater
Leaves

Suggested Ages
Seven to twelve

Lesson

STAINED GLASS WINDOWS

When your children first come back to school in September, they are still thinking "summer time" and it's a good idea to do lessons in short breaks for the first two weeks.

Making stained glass windows with fall leaves is an activity which gives your students a "hands-on" project between their lessons.

If possible, have a helper with you in the classroom for this lesson. On the first day of school, ask students to bring in fall leaves in all colors and sizes.

HINT: Some children may not live in an area where such leaves are available, so ask those who do to bring in a grocery bag of leaves to share.

Picture frame: Provide each student with a 10" x 12"-sheet of paper in a fall color. The frame will measure 1 1/2" from outside to inside. (See illustration.)

Have students cut out the inside to form the frame. Remind them to write their name on the lower right-hand corner of their frame.

Older students may begin to grate old crayons into a bowl. Use a separate bowl for each color. Younger students will need an aide to do this. Good colors are: green, orange, yellow and brown.

Give each student two sheets of waxed paper 10" x 12" and show them how to arrange their leaves on the paper. Suggest they use a mixture of colors such as green leaves mixed with reds and golds.

Select a place in the classroom with a flat surface and an outlet for your iron. Be sure the iron is old as the wax from the crayons can stick and be hard to remove. Place an old towel, doubled, on the counter surface.

In pairs, have your students walk carefully carrying their leaves on the waxed paper. If you have individual chalkboards, have them place the pictures on the board for carrying. Once students have their leaves nicely arranged on the waxed paper, they should choose three or four colors of grated crayons to sprinkle over them.

Then carefully place the second sheet of waxed paper on top of the leaves and place picture on towel and iron until crayons melt. The crayons will melt into puddles of colors over the leaves giving a stained glass look.

When students return to their desks, they will staple the frame on top of the leaves if necessary. Tape the pictures to your classroom windows for the sun to shine through.

If your class "adopts" a nursing home, or if students have "shut-in" relatives or friends, these "stained glass windows" make a thoughtful gift.

Seasonal Art

Objective
• To make an art project for Halloween

Materials
Orange construction paper
Tissue paper: orange, green and black
Glue
Pencil

Suggested Ages
Seven to twelve

Lesson

TISSUE PUMPKINS

October is a popular time of the year for students and a project aimed at Halloween is greeted enthusiastically.

Have a tissue pumpkin as a model for your students to see before they begin. See illustration.

HINT: It is much easier to purchase "Pom-Pom" tissue than to cut up the tissue found in school supply rooms. Pom-Pom tissues come in small packages and you'll only need to cut these into fourths.

Each student will need a 10" x 12"-piece of orange construction paper. Older students may draw the eyes, nose and mouth. Younger students will need help or you can provide them with a pattern. See page 133 of Teacher Resources for pattern.

You'll need large amounts of orange tissue cut into squares, a smaller quantity of black for the eyes, nose and mouth, and some green tissue for the stem.

Have students place newspaper on their desks before starting this project because the glue gets messy. Give each student a 2" x 2"-piece of construction paper with a puddle of glue in the middle.

Students take a piece of orange tissue, wrap it around the end of a pencil, dip the bottom into the glue and stick it on the pumpkin. This continues until the entire surface of the pumpkin is covered with either orange, black or green tissues.

The project will take several days and can be done when classroom work is finished. As each pumpkin is completed, have the student attach tape to the back and place it on the classroom windows for the month of October before taking it home for Halloween.

Objectives

• To provide joy in creating art projects for Christmas
• To help students understand the pleasure of creating and sharing with others

Materials

One cardboard toilet paper cylinder for each child
Red construction paper
Gold twine
Glitter
Glue
A copy of each student's class picture

Suggested Ages

Six to ten

Lesson

A CHRISTMAS ORNAMENT

If possible, arrange to have a Christmas tree in your classroom each year. This will provide you with a showcase when students create art projects to decorate the tree. Here is a simple one which parents like to receive.

Ask your students to bring in cardboard toilet paper cylinders for this project. Before beginning, show a model of one you've already made. (See illustration.)

Have your students cut out a piece of red construction paper to wrap around the cylinder. Use clear tape to attach the

Seasonal Art

ends in the back. The students should punch a small hole on each side of the top. Provide them with ten inches of gold twine to serve as the hanger on the tree. Run the twine through the holes and tie.

Have students paste their classroom pictures on the front and center of the cylinder, then run a line of glue around the picture to form a frame. Dusting the glue with glitter creates a festive Christmas ornament.

Ask your students to hang them on the tree for everyone to enjoy until Christmas vacation when they will take them home as a gift for their families.

Objectives
• To have experience working with several art mediums
• To learn to create a gift to share with another

Materials
Egg shells
Small plate or saucer
Plastic flower and leaf
Gold spray
Glue

Suggested Ages
Seven to twelve

Lesson

A CHRISTMAS PLATE

Every child delights in creating an object of beauty to present to "that special someone" in their life.

Each child will need to bring a plate to school. A good size is a saucer. Remind students they are not to bring antiques or a special family plate, but an old one which won't be missed. They should also look for a plastic flower and leaf for this project. It should be something the family can do without.

Ask them to also begin to save egg shells. Explain that they should rinse the shells well and place them on a folded paper towel to dry before bringing to school. They are not to crush the shells, but keep them in large pieces.

Have a Christmas plate to display to your students before they begin. (See illustration.)

Insist that students place newspapers on their desks before beginning this lesson. This is a project which can go on for several days. Let them work at their own pace after completing school work.

Each child can share a bottle of white glue with a partner. Have your students set the plates on their desks along with several egg shells. Tell them to make a 2" x 2" puddle of glue on the edge of the plate and smear it around to form a thin layer. While waiting for the glue to get tacky, they break off small pieces of egg shell about the size of their index finger-nail. Students continue placing glue in a small area and adding more shells.

As soon as the glue "sets up," they will layer the pieces of egg shell onto the plate beginning at the edge. All shells should overlap to give a mosaic appearance.

Students are to leave only the small area in the center of the plate open to glue the flower there. Let the plates dry for at least two days before spray painting.

All spraying should be done outside and a parent should be available to work with small groups on this part of the project. This will keep children from spraying each other for Christmas!

HINT: Use a large cardboard box (open on one side only) for spraying. Put plates inside to catch excess spray and then touch them up as needed.

Some students enjoy putting glitter on the plate after it has been sprayed. They will ask if they may bring in spray and glitter to share and this is fine.

After the project is finished, tell students they can go to the dime store and purchase a plate hanger so the plate can hang on the wall.

The final step is to have them bring in wrapping paper and ribbon to wrap their projects. An added touch is a handmade Christmas gift card to place on top of the package.

HINT: Some parents, ten years later, tell me this precious gift from their child still hangs on their wall.

TIMELY TIP: **Some children may come from homes where plates, flowers, and egg shells are not available. You might ask students who have extras to share them and have some extras on hand yourself so no child will be left out. Old saucers and plastic flowers can be purchased for very little at thrift stores. Those you do not use this year can be put aside for next.**

Seasonal Art

Objectives
• To teach students to produce colorful pictures
• To make art enjoyable

Materials
Construction paper
Crayons
Popcorn
Glue

Suggested Ages
Six to ten

Lesson

A BLOOMING TREE FOR SPRING

One of the most enjoyable times of the year is the coming of spring. As flowers begin to bloom, trees bud and leaves appear, let your students join in this awakening of nature through art with a project that will result in a wonderful art display for Open House.

Provide your students with a model to show them how the picture they will construct is made. (See illustration.)

Give each student a 12" x 18"-piece of light blue construction paper and scraps of brown and green paper.

Explain that they will cut a tree trunk and limbs from the brown paper to paste onto their blue sheet of construction paper. From the green paper they'll cut leaves and grass for their picture, then complete it with colorful flowers drawn on construction paper and pasted onto the tree. Younger children might need a pattern to follow.

Some students may wish to combine crayon flowers and grass along with the cut outs. To complete the picture, explain they will paste popcorn on the branches to represent the blossoms coming out on the trees.

This is a project which, once started, can be done by students independently over a period of days and not simply set aside for "Friday art."

Chapter 7

Go on a Paperwork Diet

- Chalkboard Activities

- Files

- Storing

- Plastic Trays

- When Students Grade Papers

- Using an Overhead Projector

Go on a Paperwork Diet

Objectives
- To control paperwork
- To get parents to help with paperwork
- To keep the upper hand over paper and to store items efficiently

Materials
Individual chalkboards
Chalkboard paint
Sorting file
Expandable file
Construction paper
File cabinet
Crayons
Hangers
Rod
Trays
Marlite® board

Next to classroom management, the second most demanding aspect of teaching is paperwork. Here are some ideas to help you manage the flood of papers which may threaten to inundate you.

CHALKBOARD ACTIVITIES

Consider making individual chalkboards for your students. Purchase quarter-inch plywood, cut boards into 12-inch squares, sand edges and spray with special chalkboard paint available at paint stores.

Chalkboards can be used in class to review spelling words, do math facts and practice handwriting. Give yourself a break from grading endless papers by having your students do their math facts on their chalkboards, hold them up for your approval and move on. Your students will get instant feedback while you take a break from your daily routine.

Individual chalkboards can also serve as portable desks when going on bus or walking field trips. Have students place chalk and chalkboard eraser in a plastic sandwich bag to take along.

TIMELY TIP: **When teachers retire they are anxious to give things away. Look for chalkboards they may have. Also, some teachers have collected enough erasers and chalk for each child to have one. Let retiring teachers know what you need; they are usually pleased to share.**

FILES

There are all types of files for controlling paperwork. Most of these are used in the business world but can be put to equally good use in your classroom.

Sorting

The SORT-ALL® is a narrow file with long narrow cardboard dividers arranged by alphabet, months of the year and by numbers. It is inexpensive and does not take up a great deal of room. Use one to keep track of classroom papers.

The expandable file is a metal file which can be opened out like an accordion and used for sorting up to 30 pages. It works well on top of a long table or shelf and can be used by students.

Both files are useful when sorting things into alphabetical order for report cards, parent conference forms, folders for parent conferences and deficiency notices.

STORING

School: Teachers have to be collectors in order to provide their students with a multitude of information often not supplied by the district.

Dittos can be found quickly when placed in color coded folders made from construction paper. Decide upon the colors you want such as: blue for reading, red for math and yellow for language.

If possible, obtain a metal file cabinet through your district. If not, look for one at garage sales, your state surplus property office (see State Government listings in your telephone book) or at discount stores. It is almost impossible to get through the years as a teacher without a file cabinet.

Larger items such as posters can be placed on skirt hangers, color coded, numbered and hung from a rod in your classroom closet. If you do not have a closet, ask your principal if you could have the custodian put a dowel rod in the back of your room where you can hang posters.

Bulletin board items can be kept from year to year in large envelopes. These can

be made from 12" x 18" sheets of construction paper with edges secured by staples. Note subject and title on outside and file in a large drawer.

Home: Usually teachers never have enough room at school for storage. One of the handiest ways to keep things at home is in the garage if you have one. For detailed information on how to build a garage storage unit, see page 134 in the Teacher Resource section.

Plastic Trays

Continue your color coding by purchasing colored plastic trays to match your reading, math and language folders. This will make it easier to collect and grade your homework and seatwork.

All math homework, for instance, would be placed in the red tray, and reading the blue one. Most trays are stackable and take up very little room.

Go on a Paperwork Diet

GRADING PAPERS

Teachers mean well and try hard, yet they never seem to get caught up with the paperwork. Some teachers carry home the same stack of papers every night for three weeks without grading them. Instead, have your students grade class work (but not tests) in school. Students benefit most from prompt feedback and it saves you from tedious, repetitious work.

Here are two ways to have students grade papers. Have them exchange papers with a neighbor. Each student will then color over all answers in yellow crayon before you repeat the answers. Then they cannot change answers.

An alternative is to have them grade their own. Explain that you know they will want to change a wrong answer but they shouldn't. Let them know the temptation will be there to cheat but it is important to be honest as they will only hurt themselves later on taking a test.

TIMELY TIP: **When school begins, send out a letter requesting parent help. Some who work will be willing to grade papers at home. You'll need to send home a Teacher's Edition and directions as to what you want them to do. Send a Grade checker and ask them to note grade in red at top of page. Be sure to let them know how much you appreciate their help.**

DIRECT CLASSROOM INSTRUCTION

Overhead Projector

The overhead projector is a fantastic way to teach. While working with it, you are giving out information and at the same time maintaining direct eye contact with your students.

Use brightly colored pens and have your students use paper and colored crayons. Recent studies indicate that students learn more when bright colors are used. If doing a language lesson, for example, use a color code for parts of speech and underline verbs in red, subject in blue and so on. Students will do the same at their desks. Children particularly enjoy this type of activity where they work along with you. You can do similar lessons in reading and math. No need to correct as this is a practice lesson.

Marlite® Board or Polar White Bristle® (Shower Board)

You may wish to cover one of your chalkboards with Marlite® Board and use colorful grease pens for doing direct teaching. The board is easy to clean and can be used in all subjects.

Chapter **8**

Classroom Helper Hints

- Cross-Age Tutors
- Parent Volunteers
- Student Helpers

Classroom Helper Hints

Objectives
* To find extra help for your classroom
* To use cross-age tutors
* To give suggestions for getting parents to help in the classroom
* To suggest that students create committees to do jobs in the room

Running a classroom is similar to being CEO of a mini-corporation. It'll be very helpful to get as many people involved as you can. Here are just a few suggestions which have worked well for other teachers.

CROSS-AGE TUTORS

When using cross-age tutors, it is best if you're a primary teacher to ask for student helpers from the intermediate grades.

If you teach fourth grade, try to obtain tutors from the sixth grade. Younger students enjoy looking up to and working with older students and it motivates them to work harder.

If you teach in a district which has early/late reading (this means half the class comes early and the others arrive an hour later), then you will find it easier to use cross-age tutors.

For example, if half your readers arrive at 8:30 in your second grade room, you can ask for an intermediate tutor. This would be, perhaps, a fifth grader

who does not ordinarily come for reading until 9:30. The student might be willing to come at 8:30 and be a cross-age tutor in your room.

At the end of the day when your late readers stay until, for example, 3 o'clock, ask for an intermediate student who came early for reading and is ready to go home at two o'clock. Maybe this student would be willing to stay an additional hour tutoring in your classroom.

If all your students come at the same time for reading each day, some teachers are still willing to let a student tutor come to your room for twenty minutes during the day, especially a gifted student who masters assignments rapidly and becomes bored easily.

If you're unable to make arrangements at your own school for a tutor, perhaps you can arrange with a nearby junior high or high school to send you students for a few hours a week. Some schools offer their students credits for this service.

If you can use cross-age tutors, train them thoroughly before they begin. This should take no more than a half hour. First discuss their responsibility to be there, to be on time and to be professional. Talk to the older students about being positive role models to your younger students.

Next describe what they will be doing. Show them the special box or shelf you have designated for them. Explain that this is where you'll put lesson plans for them (just as you do for a substitute teacher) so they need not disturb you when they walk in.

Tutors can do many of the following chores for you: help students in reading or with math facts, sort and/or grade papers, pass out homework and do bulletin boards.

Plan some reward system and be sure they know about it so they will continue coming. This can be a trip to a fast-food place, free cupcakes when a sale is being held at school or a coupon to go on their own to an eatery in your area.

PARENT VOLUNTEERS

Let parents and even grandparents know right from the start of school that you need their help. Send a note home and discuss it at your Back To School Night. With so many parents working, it is difficult to get helpers in the classroom. However, you could ask some to sign up to grade papers at home or sign up for one hour a week or month, to help tutor, do bulletin boards or assist with your physical education program. See page 135 in Teacher Resources for a "Request for Parent-Help Letter" which you may duplicate.

TIMELY TIP: **Send home a checklist to discover what skills or hobbies your children's parents have. This way you can match their interests to your classroom program. If a father is an avid fisherman, for example, he might be willing to share his expertise when you do a unit on fish. Perhaps another parent enjoys doing art projects. Gear a lesson around this interest when the parent can come and help.**

Classroom Helper Hints

STUDENT HELPERS

You'll want your students to learn responsibility as well as academic subjects. Remember there are always many jobs to be done in a classroom filled with students. Assign a committee to put up bulletin boards, another to bring suggestions to the group for art projects and another to suggest Physical Education activities.

Other jobs might be a committee to welcome new students to the classroom. This could include being sure the desk for the child is ready with pencils, paper, scissors and books and having them show the new student around the campus.

Also, elect or appoint a committee to be responsible for planning classroom parties and arranging for cleanup afterwards. Finally, if you keep animals in your classroom, a committee should be formed to be responsible for getting food for the animals, cleaning out cages and making arrangements for the animals to be kept in homes during holidays. By using a variety of committees, you'll help yourself run a more efficient and successful classroom.

For more information on how to provide job opportunities for your students, see Chapter Five in *How to Organize and Run a Successful Classroom*.

Chapter 9

Teacher Time Savers

- Classroom Time Savers
- Classroom Stamps
- Grading Papers
- Number, Please!
- Split-Class Time Saver
- Closing Your Classroom in June
- One Day at a Time

Teacher Time Savers

Objectives
- To make your teaching day easier
- To describe how to make a daily journal

Materials
Electric pencil sharpener
Name stamp
Classroom stamps
Grader
Cassette tape recorder and tape
9" x 7" binder, three-ring
8 1/2" x 5 1/2" paper, lined
Paper clips, colorful
Pen, bright color

There are many items available today that offer shortcuts and save you time. Here are some suggestions.

ELECTRIC PENCIL SHARPENER

Purchase an electric pencil sharpener. Choose one which will sharpen both primary and intermediate number 2 pencils. They are expensive — $70 to $90 — but work well, last forever and can save you time, annoyance and headaches while dealing with wall sharpeners.

NAME STAMP

During your years as a teacher, you'll write your name *thousands* of times on report cards, deficiency notices and other messages. Have a name stamp made and splurge on a self-inking stamp. This will help keep your name legible and save you from writer's cramp!

CLASSROOM STAMPS

One convenient and quick way to get messages home is to put notes on students' papers. Stamping your message can save many minutes. Your cross-age tutors or students can also use them. Here are a couple of stamps which work well in the classroom.

For more information on ordering stamps, see Teacher Resources page 137.

GRADING PAPERS

You'll spend *hours* grading papers during your tenure as a teacher. Get as much help as you can. Grading calculators designed with the teacher in mind are now available. They calculate percentages, average scores and provide a class average score. The calculator also has letter keys for all grades. Price varies from $40 to $50.

You can also find inexpensive cardboard graders at teacher stores. They are handy for you and for parent volunteers who might grade papers.

NUMBER, PLEASE!

To facilitate placing grades in your grade book, assign each of your students a number. Ask them to write the number and circle it at the top of each page of work they turn in to you.

They should write their names as well, but some students have such poor penmanship that it is difficult to decipher their names. The number is easier to read and quicker to locate in your grade book.

SPLIT-CLASS TIME SAVER

Here is an idea which works well for giving a weekly spelling test, especially in a split class. For example, if you have a third-fourth split with only seven students in the fourth grade, you would use this method with the fourth graders.

When you write your lesson plans each week, take a moment to dictate (s-l-o-w-l-y) the spelling words for the fourth graders' test into a cassette tape recorder. Be sure to remind students (on the tape) to put their names and numbers on their tests.

Before the first test, explain to the students that each Friday the cassette will be on a table in the back of the room with an earplug so they do not disturb you as you test the third graders. Assign one student to get everything ready, including the cassette machine, a list of students taking the test and a small figurine of some sort. After finishing the test and rewinding the recorder, each student will cross his or her name off the list, then place the figurine on the desk of the next student to show the recorder is free. Designate a place where the test should be placed to be graded. Students enjoy taking spelling tests on their own because it increases their sense of maturity and responsibility.

Teacher Time Savers

CLOSING YOUR CLASSROOM IN JUNE

Bringing the school year to an end can be hectic. An added complication arises if you must move to another school.

For ideas on how to successfully close your classroom, see Teacher Resources, pages 136 and 137.

ONE DAY AT A TIME

Your mind was never meant to be a bulletin board. Instead of trying to remember everything, be sure to record your meetings, purchases and miles driven for school on paper.

Preparing a Yearly Journal

Most commercial journals are simply too small for a teacher's lifestyle, so create your own! Purchase a 9" by 7" binder with three rings. Be sure it has pockets for items such as paper clips, stick 'um notes, pencil with string attached to the notebook and envelope for keeping receipts. Buy three packages of 8 1/2" x 5 1/2" three-hole, lined paper.

Take a manila folder and cut a page the same size as the paper. Punch out three holes. Type the following message on the front of the manila page:

IF FOUND, PLEASE RETURN TO:
Mrs. Mary Jones (Your name)
Telephone (200) 555-6060
in Los Angeles, CA 90015
Please call collect if out-of-town.

Look for a small calendar which has all twelve months of the current year and one for the following year, too. Fasten to the other side of the manila page.

Place 100 pages of lined paper in the binder. Use one page for each day and write the day and date for the next three months. Always use colorful pens to keep your journal cheerful.

Make two or more manila dividers for "School Business," "Goals" and "Miscellaneous," for listing addresses, telephone numbers, birthdays and other lists, such as books to order. Add fifteen pages to each of these divisions.

Next, attach your colorful pen to the notebook for safe keeping. Attach paper clips to the pocket to fasten bulletins and agendas for meetings to the appropriate day.

List your weekly yard duty and bus assignments at the top of each journal page. As you move through the days and weeks, continue to list yard duty days and times, meetings to attend and days you'll be showing a film so you'll remember to sign up for the projector.

Under "School" list the date and price of all purchases for your classroom. Also, note the odometer reading when you leave school for meetings and note again when you arrive at the meeting. An ongoing journal is essential if you're ever audited by the IRS.

One way to accomplish goals in life is to list four or five under the "Goals" section in the journal. Only one person in twenty writes down goals, yet studies show these people achieve much more than those who merely think about them. Update this section each January first. Look at your goals once a week and add to your list during the year. Date your goals and cross them out as you achieve each one. This will give you a feeling of success.

As a final touch, pick out a beautiful sticker such as an apple, bird or animal and stick it on the upper right corner of the binder. This way you'll always know the front of the binder when you pick it up. The bright sticker will also give you a good feeling each time you see it.

For the journal to be a time saver, you must use it each day. The first thing in the morning, open your journal to the correct date. Read the list of things to do that day. Look back to the day before to see if you've accomplished everything you listed. If not, write down the "still to do" items on today's page. Then rip out the old page.

Do not carry any "to do" items more than four days. A study indicated that if you delay more than four days, the project probably is of little interest to you.

Teachers who use a journal consider it one of their most valuable resources and would never leave the house without it. Let your journal work for you and give your mind a rest.

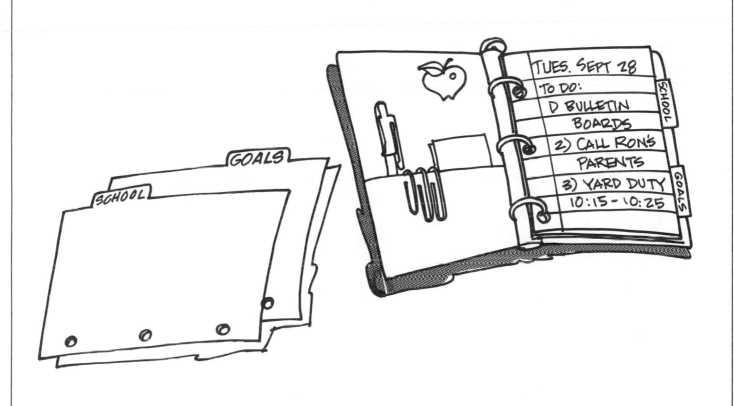

Notes

Chapter 10

Cooking in the Classroom

- Pumpkin Seeds
- Baked Pumpkin
- Chocolate Chip Cookies
- Raffling Off
- Ice Cream

Cooking in the Classroom

Objectives
- To provide students with an opportunity to enjoy cooking
- To teach students measurement
- To help students understand estimation
- To teach students to count

Materials
Portable oven or microwave
Pumpkin
Butter, knife and fork
Seasonings
Brown sugar
Ingredients for cookies
Chocolate chips
Cookie sheets and spatula
Pot holders and toothpicks
Ingredients for ice cream
Six-oz. metal cans
Milk cartons
Tongue depressors
Crushed ice
Rock salt
Paper towels
Timer
Mixing bowls and spoons

Lesson

Cooking teaches students important skills such as measurement, temperature and telling time. It's also a hands-on activity which most students thoroughly enjoy — especially eating the results!

Students are often willing to bring in milk, eggs and sugar for cooking lessons. In warm weather, consider making a freezer of ice cream. In cooler weather, bake simple recipes such as chocolate chip cookies, brownies or cupcakes.

Check with your principal before you bring in any electrical equipment. Fire Department rules change frequently. Be sure you are permitted to cook in your classroom. You might ask your PTA to provide you with a portable oven, ask for a donation from a parent or watch for a small, inexpensive portable oven at garage sales or a thrift store.

TIMELY TIP: **Use a long table in the front of the room when doing a cooking lesson. Have students write their names on slips of paper, then draw names and assign jobs such as "wash pumpkin seeds" or "break two eggs" or "stir cookie dough fifty times while class counts aloud." They love this.**

PUMPKIN SEEDS

During October plan several cooking lessons using pumpkins. Counting seeds is one way of teaching your students number sequence, particularly in the primary grades.

Bring a medium-sized pumpkin to school. In order to use the pumpkin for two lessons, cut it in half, remove and wash all seeds and place them on a towel to dry for 30 minutes. Wrap the pumpkin and keep in the refrigerator until you have time for the next lesson.

During math period do a lesson on counting. Tell the class that while they are working, you'll be baking the pumpkin seeds.

Place the seeds on a metal tray and bake at 350 degrees for twenty minutes. When they are golden brown, remove and dust lightly with a seasoning such as garlic salt.

To make the lesson more interesting, have groups estimate how many seeds there are. Have the leader write the group name on the slip and the estimate. After all seeds have been counted, the group closest to the exact number gets to draw something from your classroom "Goodie Bag." This is a brown paper bag filled with inexpensive items such as comic erasers, colorful pencils and small coin purses.

Cut up paper towels and place on students' desks. Pass out pumpkin seeds to each student and tell them to chew on the seed and discard the hull. Remind them to wait until all have been served.

BAKED PUMPKIN

Later in the week, bake the pumpkin. First have each individual or group estimate how many three-inch-square servings, for example, are in the pumpkin, and write down the estimate.

During the morning, bake the pumpkin. To improve the taste, dot the pumpkin flesh with butter and brown sugar, then dust with cinnamon, nutmeg and ground ginger. Bake on a cookie sheet at 375 degrees for about one hour. Fork test to be sure it is tender before removing from oven. Allow to cool until slightly warm.

Take the pumpkin to the front of the room and cut into sufficient serving chunks for your classroom. Pass out paper towels and serve. Count the number of servings. Again the individual or group with the nearest correct answer wins a prize out of the "Goodie Bag." (They don't have to eat the pumpkin, but encourage them to give it a try.)

Cooking in the Classroom

CHOCOLATE CHIP COOKIES

Another way to teach measurement and temperature is to bake cookies. Chocolate Chip cookies are easy to make and most students relish eating them.

Use the recipe found on the back of the bag. If you wish, double the dough recipe but put in one bag of chocolate chips to save money. Assign students to bring in the necessary ingredients during the week you'll be baking. Give them hints ahead of time on how they can bring one egg or a cup of sugar to school without breaking or spilling it. This teaches them both sharing and responsibility.

One way of doing this lesson is to use small groups. You can have one group to collect all ingredients; another to collect all pans, timers and cups; another to mix; another to bake and finally a group to do the clean up!

After the cookies have baked and cooled, pass out paper towels and let your designated servers deliver the cookies. Insist that all students wait until everyone is served before they start eating.

RAFFLING OFF

If you have a few cookies left, consider raffling them off. Raffling is a good way to practice math and can be used for other things in class.

Those who want a second cookie gather in a circle. At the count of three, each student extends either one or two fingers of one hand. Total all the fingers. Say your total is twenty-three. Start with the teacher and count off around the circle aloud. The student who says, "Twenty-three," gets a cookie and drops out of the circle. Repeat the "raffling" process until all cookies are gone.

ICE CREAM MAKING, INDIVIDUALIZED

When the weather turns warm near the end of school, children will be enthralled by making ice cream. Rather than using a large ice cream freezer, have students make their own ice cream at their desks. Caution: Before they do, be sure they have placed newspapers on top of their desks. Rock salt can damage the surface.

This recipe will serve about eighteen students. Adjust as needed for your classroom.

Vanilla Ice Cream

> 4 eggs
> 2 1/4 cups sugar
> 6 cups milk
> 4 cups half-and-half
> 1 scant tablespoon vanilla
> 1/2 teaspoon salt

Beat eggs until light and fluffy. Add sugar slowly and stir well. Add milk and cream, stir. Add vanilla and salt, beat well.

Utensils and other items you'll need:

> Mixing bowl, preferably glass
>   so students can see
> Glass measuring cups
> Measuring spoons
> Rubber spatula
> Wooden spoon or hand beater
> Rock salt, five pounds
> Crushed ice, at least three,
>   seven-pound bags

Large pan for crushed ice
Plastic wrap
Bowl for rock salt

For each student:

> 1 tongue depressor
> 1-6 oz. metal juice can (thoroughly washed and paper label removed if necessary)
> 1 half-gallon milk carton (thoroughly rinsed)
> Cut milk carton so it is 1/2" shorter than the juice can. (See illustration.)

Directions:

At a large table in the front of the room, mix ingredients in glass mixing bowl. As an added attraction, have students volunteer to beat for fifty seconds and use a timer. Others can crack eggs, measure sugar and milk.

Cooking in the Classroom

After the ice cream mixture is thoroughly blended, move to the sink in your room. Place crushed ice in a large pan and rock salt in a bowl. Have small squares of plastic wrap available to cover cans so rock salt won't fall inside.

Call two students at a time and have them fill their juice cans 3/4 full with the ice cream mixture, then cover (temporarily) with plastic wrap. Next the students take their milk cartons and place one handful of ice in the bottom and sprinkle one tablespoon of rock salt on top of the ice.

SUGGESTION: Prior to this lesson explain to your students that salt is added to the ice to lower the freezing point of the water below 32 degrees Fahrenheit. It therefore freezes the ice cream more rapidly.

After placing the juice cans on the layer of ice, students continue layering ice and rock salt until the carton is full. For every handful of crushed ice, sprinkle one tablespoon of rock salt.

Back at their desks, each student should remove the plastic wrap from the top of their can and stir the mixture with the tongue depressor. It will take from five to ten minutes to freeze, depending upon the room temperature. The ice will melt and students may need to add more ice and salt during the stirring time to keep the freezing process going. After the ice cream is frozen, the students use the tongue depressors to eat it.

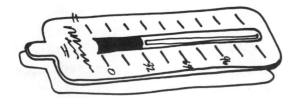

TIMELY TIP: **Many students will get very excited as soon as they see the first indication of frozen ice cream on their tongue depressor. Alert them to this ahead of time. They need to know that they are not to start eating until the mixture is nearly solid.**

Chapter 11

Computer Wise

- Four Ways to Obtain Computers
- Using a Computer in the Classroom
- A Roving Computer
- Computer Software

Computer Wise

Objectives
• To incorporate computers into your classroom curriculum
• To suggest ways to obtain computers and computer software
• To establish a workable process for scheduling students for computer time

Materials
3" x 5" cards
Timer
Computer
Computer software
Computer catalogs

The computer not only teaches students to read, write and do math but keeps them motivated at the same time. Many students will beg to go to the computer lab and work. Harness this eagerness, to teach your students the basics and beyond.

"But I don't *have* a computer," you say. Some school districts have been able to get computer labs either through parent participation or federal involvement, but if you are still computerless, here are some strategies.

WRITE A GRANT: Some teachers apply for grants for the extra money needed to purchase a computer. One teacher was able to obtain seventeen computers, software and a printer this way. Look on page 137 in Teacher Resources for information on writing grants.

INCENTIVES PROVIDED BY GROCERY STORES: Some grocery chains devote public relations and sales promotion efforts to getting computers for local schools. These stores exchange grocery cash register tapes from their stores for money for computers, software and printers. If this is true in your area, draft your students to mount an effective campaign to collect cash register tapes.

FEDERAL GOVERNMENT: If you teach in an area with a high welfare population, you might contact the federal Department of Education to see if your school qualifies for computers. Many schools have successfully acquired computers this way.

BOOK PUBLISHERS: If your district is getting ready to adopt a new math series, volunteer to pilot the math program. When you do this, ask for all computer software which comes with the program as well as the books.

COMPUTER IN THE CLASSROOM

If you have only one computer, you must arrange a schedule which will give time to each student each week.

For example, you may choose to have math period only set aside for the computer or you might decide to schedule students during the entire day. Take five 3" x 5" cards and label one Monday, the next Tuesday and through the week. Decide upon the amount of time you wish each student or pair of students to have on the computer. Then list the names for each day and times. Post the card near the computer. Be sure each child has a turn on the computer sometime during the week.

A ROVING COMPUTER

When schools have only a few computers, it is more efficient and easier to move the computer when one is assigned to each wing. Teachers on that wing then meet and agree upon a schedule as to how long the computer will be in a classroom.

Computers are sensitive and care must be taken when they are moved. It is best for a teacher to move a computer rather than students.

TIMELY TIP: If you don't often have access to a computer, you might wish to arrange for computer time both before and after school. This is most useful when students ride the bus and arrive early. One teacher who was scheduled for the computer only during the month of March did this. She also asked some students to arrive early and tutor students who had never used the computer before. This meant she was free to get the room ready for the entire class before school actually started.

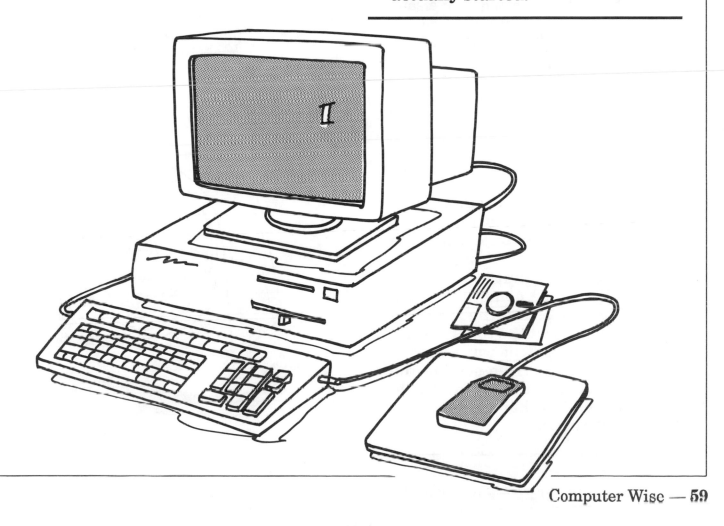

Computer Wise

COMPUTER SOFTWARE

Schools and teachers are being flooded with catalogs on available computer software. Check with your principal or secretary to find where these catalogs are kept. Also, many districts now have computer software, videos, slides and movies as part of their Audio-Visual programs.

Whatever your source, be sure copying is permitted before you copy software. Some material is public domain but some is copyrighted. Check before you begin.

A list of software, along with a sample keyboard to copy for classroom use, can be found on pages 137 and 138 in Teacher Resources.

TIMELY TIP: **At the beginning of the computer period, on a timer next to the computer, set the amount of time the first pair will have. Call the first students on your list to the computer. After the timer goes off, the first students will reset the timer for the next students. This way you stop some students from setting the timer for extra time for themselves while other students get shortchanged.**

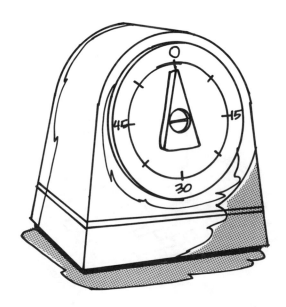

Chapter 12

Physical Education Ideas

- Deck Rings
- Hoops
- Jump Ropes
- Parachute Games

Physical Education Ideas

Objectives
• To enhance the elementary school Physical Education program
• To create Physical Education equipment
• To make the Physical Education program fun for students

Materials
Deck rings
PVC pipe
Dowel rods
Rope
Plastic tape
Glue
Duct tape
Volleyball net
Chalkboard eraser
Parachute

Suggested Ages
Five to twelve

Lesson

DECK RINGS

Both primary and intermediate students enjoy playing with deck rings. These soft rubber rings resembling seven-inch donuts are held between the thumb and forefinger and tossed. They cost only a couple of dollars each and can be purchased at sporting goods stores. If there are none in stock, ask them to order a half dozen for you.

In the primary grades, line up your students in pairs with partners facing each other about four feet apart. Let them take turns tossing a ring back and forth to each other. This helps improve their eye-hand coordination. As they gain more expertise, have them move farther apart.

In the intermediate grades, string a net between two volley ball poles. Have your students select two teams and explain you'll be playing by volley ball rules. This means the server will stand in the back and will be given two chances to get the ring over the net. If the first serve fails, the server has one more chance.

The first team to reach twenty-one points is declared the winner. Students in the upper grades, particularly, enjoy playing this game and will ask to play it again and again. They become most proficient tossing the ring high into the air, spiking it and catching their opponents off guard.

HOOPS

You may buy or make hoops for your students. To make, purchase 3/4"-PVC pipe at a plumbing store. The length should be three times the diameter of the finished hoop. A 30"-diameter is a good size for kindergarten through intermediate classes, so you'd purchase 90" for one hoop.

To assemble, purchase doweling to fit snugly inside the pipe. Cut the doweling into 1 1/2" pieces, coat with white glue and insert inside the open ends of the pipe. Push the two ends of the pipe together and finish by covering the seam with duct tape.

HAPPY HOOPS

You'll discover many uses for your hoops depending upon your grade level. Kindergartners can be taught to follow directions while sitting in the middle of the hoops as shown here.

You can give directions such as: "At the count of three, stand up." Or "Jump up, bend over and put one leg and one arm outside the hoop." Or, "Jump up and down inside your hoop while we all count to ten."

Primary students, particularly, enjoy going out and rolling the hoops on a windy day. They also like to be timed to see who can keep a hoop rolling the longest.

Line your students up in a clear area of the blacktop. Be sure they are spaced apart and do this in small groups. Stand where they can see you and tell them you'll count to three and then they can begin to roll their hoops. Remind them to follow their hoops while you keep track of the time. If you wish, tell them the top three rollers will roll again for the final competition.

Hoops can also be used on the blacktop with students standing inside them to do exercises. This confines them to one area and helps to keep the group organized.

Primary students also enjoy using the hoops as jump ropes. For a free-play activity, let them skip with their hoops across the playground.

Hoops can also be placed on the blacktop in two, three or more rows. (See the illustration.) The teams should line up behind a designated line and they can either jump or hop from hoop to hoop or run a slalom race around the hoops. To make it more exciting, in the last hoop place a chalkboard eraser which they must pick up and pass to the next person in line. That student, in turn, will place the eraser in the last hoop before returning to his or her place in line.

For more information on hoop lessons, see page 137 in Teacher Resources.

Physical Education Ideas

JUMP ROPES

Students love using jump ropes. You can easily make your own from rope, have your students make them from a series of rubber bands (Chinese jump ropes) or you can buy plastic ropes.

Purchase rope at a hardware store. Cut into lengths for individual jumpers and have several longer pieces available for group jumping activities. Measure your students by taking a string and having a student stand on the middle of it. Then draw the string up under the armpits. Record the length of the string. This will tell you the right length.

Cover the ends with plastic tape to keep them from fraying. You might also want to mark them by tying blue thread around the ends, for example, so you can tell your classroom's ropes from others'.

If you're considering doing ongoing jump rope activities, you might wish to purchase sturdy plastic ropes from a supplier. Measure your students so you order the correct length. See page 137 in Teacher Resources.

You may use prepared jump rope lessons listed on page 137 in Teacher Resources to help your students learn to jump and skip rope. Also, teach techniques of skip jumping, jumping on one foot and cross overs. Many students have difficulty with these skills and your encouragement can be most helpful. Practice and be a role model of an outstanding jumper for your students. They will love this.

PARACHUTE GAMES

Students become very excited when they see a parachute. Use this natural interest to enlarge your Physical Education program. Buy booklets and tapes on parachute games to use in the classroom prior to going outside. Inside the room use a large sheet to show students how to roll the 'chute, hold it and lift it.

Once outside be sure each student knows where to stand and what to do. Parachute activities such as "Clouds," "Waves," "Popcorn" and "Mushrooms" are fun for students of all ages. (For more information on parachute activities see page 137 in Teacher Resources.)

TIMELY TIP: **If you have a problem finding an inexpensive parachute, check with your state surplus services. Airbases frequently will contribute worn parachutes to such an agency. You should be able to purchase one at a reasonable cost.**

Check with your district first for any guidelines you'll need to follow such as spraying the parachute with fire retardant, keeping it in a metal can and where to store it.

Chapter 13

Merry Measurement

- Weighing In
- Stations One to Six

Merry Measurement

Objectives
- To teach estimation
- To provide an understanding of a cup, pint and quart
- To teach weight in ounces and pounds
- To reinforce addition facts

Materials
Full can of tuna (remove label)
Full can of soup (remove label)
Potato
Five apples
Five bananas
Five oranges
75 paper clips/bowl
50 beans/bowl
Measuring cup, marked in ounces
Quart jar
Pint jar
Water
Paring knife
Three 16-oz. scales and bathroom scale

Suggested Ages
Eight to twelve

Lesson

Hands-on activities, both in the classroom and outside, pay dividends in student learning while providing a change from the basic textbook. From time to time, turn your classroom and playground into a math laboratory.

WEIGHING IN

To do this lesson, arrange six stations in your classroom. The ditto, which you may reproduce, is on page 139 in Teacher Resources. Each student should have a copy.

Students should have a partner. They may pair up on their own or you may match them up in any way that has students working with different children on different projects during the year.

Weighing-Station Names

Use construction paper to make large signs designating each station and post them.

Stations
1. People-weighing station
2. Canned goods station
3. Food-weighing station
4. Estimation station
5. Jar station
6. Fun Money station

Before beginning the lesson, explain that each student will have a ditto and pencil and will answer all questions.

SUGGESTION: To have students distributed evenly among stations, put slips numbered 1-6 in a grab bag. Have one partner from each pair draw a number. This will tell them where to begin. Explain that if they draw number five, for example, they will start with station five, then go to six, then to one and continue through four.

Tell your students that the information recorded during the lesson will be discussed in class the following day. Remind them to keep their answer sheets.

Station One: Weight Station
1. Estimate your partner's weight. Record.

Weigh your partner. How much in pounds? Record.

How many ounces would this be? Record.

Your partner does the same for you. Record.

Station Two: Canned Food Station

1. How much do you estimate the tuna weighs? Record.

   How much does it weigh in ounces? Record.

   How much would two cans weigh? Record.

2. How much do you think the soup weighs?

   How much does it weigh in ounces? Record.

   How much would three cans weigh? Record.

Station Three: Food-Weighing Table

On this table place paper towels, a paring knife, apples, oranges, bananas or other fruit. Post a sign saying "You may cut and weigh no more than six ounces of fruit to eat. You may not choose all of one fruit. You must take at least one slice of each."

NOTE: Use any two or three fruits available in season.

Station Four: Estimation Station

At this station have a one-pound scale and a large baking potato. Also, one bowl with 75 paper clips and another bowl with 50 beans.

1. Estimate the weight of the potato. Record. Weigh the potato and record.

2. Guess how many paper clips are in the bowl? Record.

3. Guess how many beans are in the bowl? Record.

   The class will count the paper clips and beans tomorrow.

Station Five: Jar Station

If possible, have this station near your sink with water available.

Provide a measuring cup, a pint and a quart jar.

1. Fill a measuring cup with water. How many ounces in a cup? Record.

2. Use the measuring cup to fill the pint jar. How many ounces in a pint? Record.

3. Now fill the quart jar. How many ounces in a quart? Record.

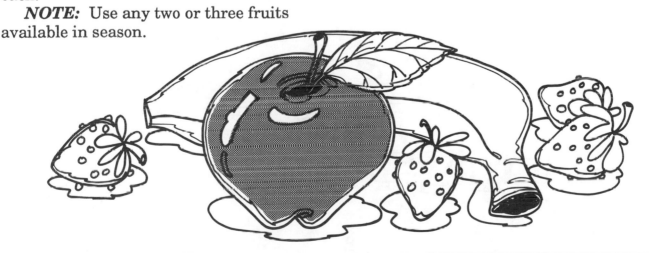

Merry Measurement

Station Six: **Fun Money Station**

As a final exercise, provide your students with a fun game using their names.

HAVE FUN WITH YOUR NAME!

Write out your full name on a piece of paper. Find out how much your name is worth. Use the code below.

a, e, i, o, u = 5 cents each
b, c, g, j, k, l, n, p, s, t, v = 4 cents each
d, f, h, m, r, w = 6 cents each
q, x, y, z = 10 cents each

My name is _____.

My name is worth _____.

My partner's name is _____.

My partner's name is worth _____.

KEEP THIS PAPER IN YOUR MATH BOOK UNTIL TOMORROW. WE WILL DISCUSS ALL ANSWERS AT THAT TIME.

Chapter 14

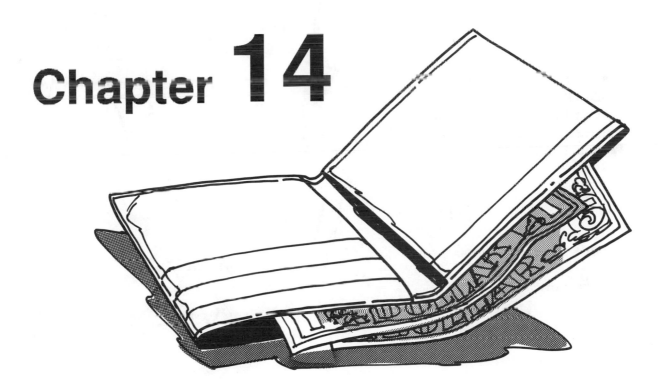

Dollars and Cents

- Counting from One to One Hundred
- Coin Values
- Using Money
- Check Writing

Dollars and Cents

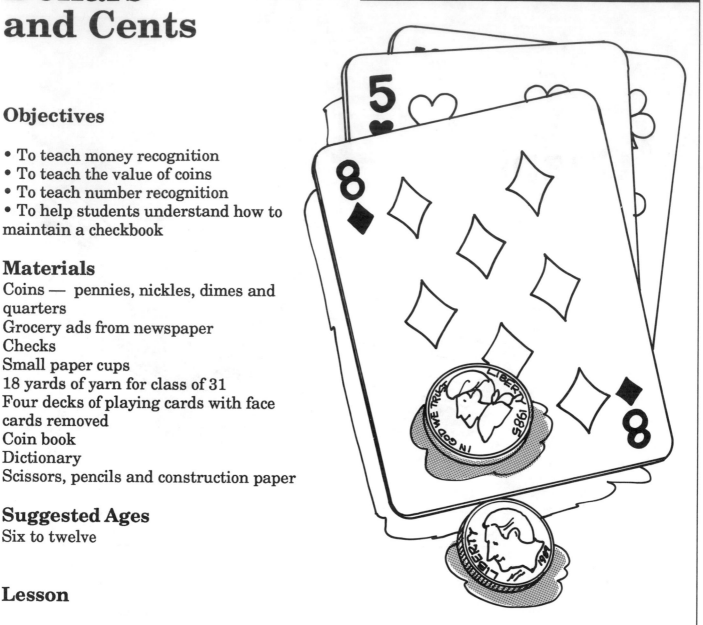

Objectives

• To teach money recognition
• To teach the value of coins
• To teach number recognition
• To help students understand how to maintain a checkbook

Materials

Coins — pennies, nickles, dimes and quarters
Grocery ads from newspaper
Checks
Small paper cups
18 yards of yarn for class of 31
Four decks of playing cards with face cards removed
Coin book
Dictionary
Scissors, pencils and construction paper

Suggested Ages

Six to twelve

Lesson

Students particularly enjoy playing cards and working with real money. You can combine these two activities, especially in the primary grades, to teach both number recognition and money sense.

Provide each student with a small paper cup containing ten pennies or have students make a circle of yarn or string on their desks and place the coins inside the circle. This provides them with a "money bank."

Pass out large playing cards using Ace through ten. Stand in front of the room and instruct your students that at the snap of your fingers, they are to pick up one penny and cover one heart, one club or whatever symbol they have on their card. Continue until all students have covered all the symbols with pennies.

Then ask your students to "raise your index finger to the sky," then zoom down. As they touch each coin, count aloud. Shuffle the cards and play again.

TIMELY TIP: **Children are much more enthusiastic when you bring in real money from the bank. Purchase several rolls of coins (such as pennies, nickles, dimes and quarters) for money lessons. Before beginning, however, explain these coins belong to you and you don't expect anyone will take them. When you keep them in paper cups, you'll have a quick method of discovering any missing coins. I've had very few losses over the years and found using real money much more helpful than cardboard coins.**

COUNTING FROM ONE TO ONE HUNDRED

Some students have a difficult time counting from one to one hundred. Here is a hint which works well. Bring 100 pennies into the classroom for these students. Have the student stand alongside a table or long shelf with scissors, pencil and construction paper. Model for the student how you want this done by cutting out one small piece of paper (about one-inch square) and writing "1" on it. Then rest a penny on the edge of the paper to weight it down. This way the slips won't blow away. Repeat with the next slip of paper

labeled "2." See illustration. Tell the student to continue doing this until he or she reaches one hundred. A student having problems should go to the dictionary and turn pages to find what number comes next. This not only frees you to help other students, it gives the child independence. After a few days most children will usually have the numbers in their proper order and be able to say them correctly.

HINT: This activity can also be done in pairs or in a group with students helping each other.

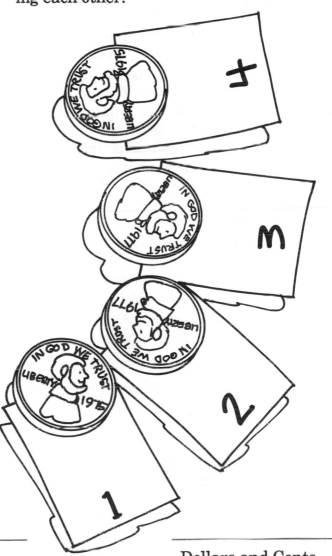

Dollars and Cents

COIN VALUES

While doing a unit on money, employ an inexpensive coin book which can be purchased at a book or coin store. Send home a note to parents telling them you'll be studying money for several days and would like them to send in one coin (not one of great worth, however) with a very old date on it.

Spend time discussing the coin book with your students. Explain how it is arranged by denomination of the coins and how to move down the page to find the date for their coin. Also explain what "Uncirculated," "Fine" and "Good" mean so they understand a worn coin will not have the value of one which has been kept in a special place and looks brand new.

After students finish their daily work, provide a place for them to go and look up the value of their coins. They'll enjoy discovering the oldest coins as well as the most valuable ones.

Also, if you as a teacher have access to a special coin, you might want to share it with your students. A gold dollar minted in 1864 in Philadelphia (and worth more than $400) brought to a classroom made a fantastic finale for the money unit.

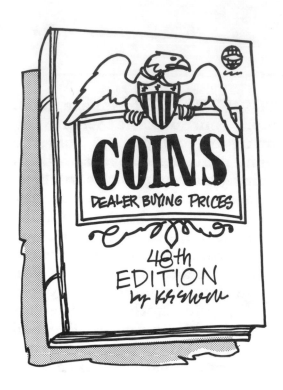

USING MONEY

Another way to teach the value of money is to combine this with a food lesson. For example, prior to Thanksgiving, have your students plan a dinner for a family of four. Tell them they will have $30 to spend for the food which should include a turkey weighing between ten and fifteen pounds, dressing, potatoes, salad, dessert and any extras they can afford. Have each student bring in grocery ads from newspapers and cut out pictures of these items with prices. Then pass out paper and have each student *write* out a menu, paste on pictures of food and enter the cost. At the bottom of the page they must total the money spent and see how much was left. Students wishing to share orally can give a brief report about their Thanksgiving dinner lesson.

CHECK WRITING

In the intermediate grades make copies of blank checks and Records of Transactions, or find someone who will bring in old unused checks for this lesson.

On the overhead or the chalkboard, list items to pay such as: house rent, food and utilities; then have students write out checks for each bill to the local company. Establish the total amount in the checkbook and have the students subtract each check. See if any have the correct balance in their checkbook when they finish.

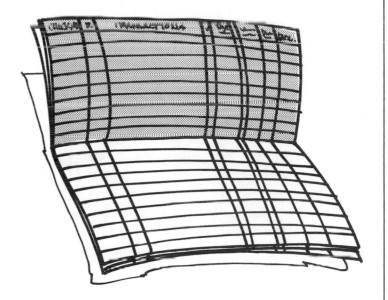

Notes

Chapter 15

Self-Esteem Builders

- Clap, Clap and Clap Again

- Using Art to Build Self-Esteem

- Providing a Loving Environment

- Class Meetings

- Individual Differences

- Choices

- Praise, Praise, Praise

- Keeping a Daily Journal

- Building Academic Self-Esteem

Self-Esteem Builders

Objectives
• To help students feel good about themselves
• To provide opportunities for children from other cultures to share their backgrounds
• To help students feel comfortable writing about their feelings

Materials
Journals

Suggested Ages
Five to twelve

Lesson

As a teacher, you are in a position not only to build but to demonstrate self-esteem in your classroom. So many students are crying out to be noticed, loved and appreciated that we cannot overlook this important part of our teaching day.

To demonstrate self-esteem, you'll need to express self-confidence and a positive feeling about yourself. You'll also need to demonstrate a positive attitude toward your class.

CLAP, CLAP AND CLAP AGAIN

When students do an outstanding job, it should be recognized as soon as possible. This can be done by teaching your students a very special clap which they will love to do.

For example, Randy had not been turning in his math homework for several weeks. After a parent conference, he did. It was time to recognize this with a big "three clap" for Randy.

Here is how it is done:
Teacher counts: "One, two, three"
Class: One giant clap
Teacher counts: "One, two, three"
Class: One giant clap
Teacher counts: "One, two, three"
Class: One final giant clap

By counting and doing one single clap together, you foil students who clap on and on trying to be silly.

Another idea is to have older students substitute finger snapping for clapping. No matter which method you use, Randy knows what he's done is appreciated.

TIMELY TIP: Be very careful about the manner in which you compliment your students. For example, Mrs. Williams had yard duty early one morning when Cassandra and her friend, Betsy arrived. Mrs. Williams said, "What a pretty pink sweater you're wearing today, Cassandra." Poor Betsy stood by and felt dreadful in her faded sweatshirt. Cassandra felt great, but Betsy felt hurt and left out.

USING ART TO BUILD SELF-ESTEEM

Have a bulletin board set aside for your students' art work. One idea is to use string to divide your largest board into paper-sized rectangles (8 1/2" x 11"), one for each child in your classroom.

Once each month, ask your students to pick out the art work they'd like to have posted in their personal square. In fact, older students can put up their own, changing it whenever they choose.

PROVIDE A LOVING ENVIRONMENT

One of the kindest things you can do on a day-to-day basis is to provide your students a loving environment. Make your room a place where you nurture and build self-esteem because this is the daily food of emotional health.

Self-esteem means students know themselves, accept themselves and, even with limitations, still believe they are worthwhile human beings.

One of the most important components of self-esteem is related to feelings. Here are a variety of ways to help your students be aware of their feelings and the feelings of others.

TIMLEY TIP: Save some of the early art work so you can show your students how much they have improved. Don't make a negative comment. Simply point out, "This is how you drew a flower in September and look at what you're doing now." Children need to see their progress and see it often in order to feel they are doing great work. Show them.

Self-Esteem Builders

CLASS MEETINGS

Class meetings conducted on a regular basis can help children feel good about themselves. Always start the meeting with students saying positive things about each other. This might be, "I want to thank Mai Lee for helping me to the office when I fell down at recess today." This will make Mai Lee feel good and will also set an example of caring for others in your children's world.

INDIVIDUAL DIFFERENCES

In our classrooms today, we have many students from different cultures. It is important that these children, their cultures and traditions be honored. Set the tone by inviting speakers of various national backgrounds to visit your classroom. Better yet, ask your students to give a report about their countries and some of the traditions.

Set aside a time for the other children to ask questions, view clothes or foods from the culture and see pictures of the native land.

CHOICES

If possible, set aside an hour every few days as "Classroom Study Time." Explain to your students that they may use this time as they choose. For example, they might 1) finish any homework so they will be free at home that night or 2) work on an art project or 3) complete their science project. Present other choices on other days. By giving children choices, you are building their confidence in their own decision-making abilities which, in turn, leads to positive self-esteem.

PRAISE, PRAISE, PRAISE

Children need generous, *sincere* praise on a daily basis. Provide this as often as you can. Tell them how much you appreciate them with emphasis on their accomplishments, actions and behavior rather than their appearance, clothes or belongings. Let them know how pleased you are to have them in your classroom. They will thrive on this attention which can help them grow into positive-thinking adults.

REMINDER: Children who like themselves like to behave themselves.

AN UNPOPULAR CHILD

If you have a child in your classroom who is not liked and is constantly picked on, there are several things you might do. First of all, in a private meeting, help the student to see how some behavior changes might lead others in the classroom to be friendlier.

If the child does make changes and is still not accepted, you'll need to talk to the entire class. You may want to send the child out of the room for some reason to give you time to discuss the situation with the class. Tell them how much Ricky, for example, is trying to improve but needs their help. Point out how wonderful it would be if they would ask him to play with them at recess and lunch.

You'll be surprised how much children want to help others to be part of their group.

For additional resources including songs on building self-esteem, look in Teacher Resources, page 142.

BUILDING ACADEMIC SELF-ESTEEM

Each May, teachers wonder if they should retain certain children. Perhaps nothing else in the school experience lowers a child's self-esteem as much as being retained. In fact, many studies indicate that retention is counter-productive.

For information on an alternative method, see Teacher Resources on pages 140 and 141.

Self-Esteem Builders

KEEPING A DAILY JOURNAL

Students need to develop their own sense that they are unique and special. One way to do this is to provide them with time to write in a Daily Journal. They can use a small, personal notebook, stapled sheets of paper you provide or even use a computer to do this on a daily basis.

Here are some questions you might use to help them begin:

1. What do you do that makes others happy? How does this make you feel?

2. What makes you feel special? Describe the feelings you get from feeling special.

3. What neat experience have you had lately which made you feel happy inside? Tell how you felt.

Chapter 16

Hail to the Chief

- The Class President
- The Vice President

Hail to
the Chief

Objectives
- To make your teaching day easier
- To explain how the use of class officers teaches leadership, builds self-esteem and demonstrates the democratic process

Suggested Ages
Six to twelve

CLASS PRESIDENT

As a teacher you'll be running a mini-corporation for nearly ten months out of the year. You cannot do it alone!

By electing a Class President, Vice President and other officers, you have students share some of the classroom chores. At the same time, they are learning leadership qualities, public speaking and decision-making skills.

Decide ahead of time what you want the President to do. For example, he or she could conduct Show and Tell in the primary grades and Sharing in the intermediate grades, giving you the opportunity to step back and rest for a few moments.

When the President is always first in line, you cut out a great deal of arguing and fighting over "I'm first today" by other students as they go to and from recess and lunch.

The Class President can also preside over oral reports in science or language while you sit at the back of the room with your grade book making notes and determining a grade.

The Vice President has three responsibilities to carry out. He or she takes over when the President is absent, conducting Show and Tell in primary grades and Sharing in intermediate. He or she takes over responsibilities for students who are absent, such as leading the Flag Salute. The Vice President is always last in line and in charge of urging tardy students to line up. He or she will be last to leave the room, checking to be sure all students are out and the door is closed.

You should be able to hold your first election by the beginning of the second month of school. In most classrooms, it works best to have the President and Vice President hold the office for one month. This way more students will have the opportunity to serve. For more information on how to arrange classroom elections for officers, see page 142 in Teacher Resources.

During the first week of school, alert your students that by the second month both a presidential and a jobs election will be conducted. Tell them you will model for them many of the jobs such as: President, Flag-Salute Leader, and Librarian.

During the first month of school, explain carefully as you conduct Show and Tell or Sharing time and organize the presentation of oral reports. The students will watch you closely and be motivated to become part of your democratically run classroom.

Chapter 17

Great Expectations

- Motivation
- Fear of Failure

Great Expectations

Objectives
• To help students want to learn
• To motivate students to do well in school
• To demonstrate the importance of enthusiasm in the classroom
• To help students overcome feelings of failure

Suggested Ages
Five to twelve

When teachers set high standards and make it clear they expect their students will achieve them, the children perform much better academically than those with teachers who set low standards.

A recent study conducted by the University of Florida showed that the combination of great expectations by teachers and high-parental expectations made a major difference in how much students learned. As we know, some parents are unwilling, unable or unavailable to work with their children. Still, even without parental support, teachers who communicate high expectations in words, body language and actions, see much higher student achievement than teachers who don't.

MOTIVATION

This is a hard-to-analyze teaching skill. The amount of learning that takes place really depends upon our students' desire to learn. It's up to us to instill that desire.

Here are some suggestions:
1. Lessons must have value. Students will do better if they understand how a specific lesson will serve them today or next week or next year. Therefore, make it a habit to preface each lesson by explaining why a child needs to learn that particular skill. This will help the student to "buy into the task."
2. Rewards are helpful. Some teachers use stickers, charts, popcorn parties or field trips.
3. Praise both by teacher and peers is most successful. This must, of course, be sincere praise which focuses on the work done. A few words of encouragement and praise make a student more eager to do a lesson, write a paper or prepare for an oral report.
4. Share your own joy of learning. Students enjoy hearing their teachers talk about their childhoods. Tell your students, for example, about the joy that knowing how to read has brought into your life. Tell a little about your most enjoyable childhood books. Explain how important you felt as you collected money on your paper route or from other jobs since you knew how to add, subtract and multiply.

TIMELY TIP: **Your enthusiasm is catching! Particularly in the primary grades, students love to please their teachers and this is a strong motive to learn. In the upper grades, the peer group becomes more important, yet teachers are still held in high esteem. Always let your students know how pleased you are when they do an assignment, finish their homework or do their best on an oral report. Your sincere enthusiasm can be a real reward.**

FEAR OF FAILURE

A number of students are afraid to try for fear they might fail. It is often wise at the start of the year to spend time talking about "New Beginnings."

Talk and role play about how it feels to be a beginner. You can relate your talk to well-known people in sports, government and the arts. Ask how a well-known sports figure might have felt the first time he or she played. Talk about feelings, explaining that they are neither good nor bad. Talk about feelings of failure. Talk about who you are as opposed to what you do.

Notes

Chapter 18

Create "Happy Happenings" in Your Classroom

- Ten Ways to Create "Happy Happenings"

Create "Happy Happenings" in Your Classroom

Objectives
• To spark curiosity and bring joy into your classroom
• To stretch your students' imaginations

Materials
Kites and string
Hoops
Books
Record player
Music records or
Cassette player and tapes
Camera and film
Movies and projector
Popcorn

Suggested Ages
Five to twelve

Lesson

No matter what your teaching situation is, bring the joy of living, learning and caring into your room. You and your students will all benefit when you make each day a "special happening."

Here are some suggestions which have worked well for other teachers:

1. Take a walking field trip to a nearby park. Point out the colors and shapes of the leaves. Have your students feel the bark on the trunks of trees and bend low and look for a bug. Ask your students: What is the tree doing? Where is the bug going? How do the leaves feel as you hold them in your hands? Do they smell?

2. Use an art lesson to design and make kites. On a windy day, go outside and fly them. Ask: How far do you think your kite could travel? Or say: Pretend your kite doesn't need a string. How far would it travel? Would you like to follow? If you and your kite could go anywhere in the whole world, where would you go?

3. As clouds fill the sky, take your students outside to lie on the ground and watch them go by. Ask: What do you see in the clouds? A horse? A castle? A rabbit?

4. Have a good supply of hula hoops. For more excitement, take your students outside on a windy day to roll their hoops. With a little push, plus wind power, the hoops will take off. Your children will race after them bubbling over with laughter. Provide your students with the joy of running with the wind.

5. Read aloud every day, offering your students the pleasure of listening to a

story. As you read, emphasize your own emotions of joy, wonder or sadness. Your students will love this. Choose a variety of books, short stories and poems to share.

6. While students do seatwork, play happy songs on your cassette player or record player. Add to your collection each year.

7. Take pictures of your students doing special things all during the school year. Be sure to photograph each student and post the snapshots on a cupboard door. Your students and visitors will have a special visual history of the year. On the final day of school, surprise your students by passing out the pictures showing them doing something special.

8. Make Fridays special days in your classroom by showing a movie or video. Bring in a large bowl of popped corn or pop some in the classroom.

9. When your students are wiggly, pull the drapes and turn off the lights. Then sit quietly and tell them a beautiful and warm story about a special time in your childhood. You'll be surprised how much they enjoy this and how calming it is.

10. From time to time, say to your students, "I'm going to give you a BIG word today." Then write the word on the chalkboard and ask them to return the next day with a definition for the word. BIG words create excitement in a classroom and students look forward to the challenge.

Here are three examples:
1. Photosynthesis
2. Paleontologist
3. Geochronology

Notes

Chapter 19

Science Speakers

- Examples of Speakers
- Where to Find Speakers
- Two Weeks Before Your Speaker's Visit
- One Week Before Your Speaker's Visit
- Three Days Before Your Speaker's Visit
- Preparing Your Students
- The Day of the Visit

Science Speakers

Objectives

• To find speakers for science units
• To explain the importance of speakers bringing "hands-on" materials for students
• To prepare your room and students for the speakers' presentations

Materials
Letter
Map to school
Pencils
Paper
Telephone book
Slide projector
Screen
Computer

In the elementary classroom, teachers are required to present six or seven lessons each day and sometimes science just gets "squeezed in." Usually teachers use the science textbook, add a film from time to time and perhaps require a written report.

One way to put real "pizazz" into your science curriculum is to invite speakers knowledgeable in the subject area your students are studying. Many teachers believe an outside speaker is an endangered species, but they are all around you if you know where to look.

EXAMPLES OF SPEAKERS

Here are four examples of exciting speakers. Notice that during their presentations, each one used eye-catching items, many of which the students could handle or even keep.

1. An entomologist (insect specialist) spoke about "bugs." His speciality was beetles and he brought several hundred he had collected in his native Mexico.

The class was allowed to handle his special net for catching bugs, a killing jar and a display container. He also showed slides and invited the students to ask questions. They were so excited they asked him to stay as long as possible.

2. A pilot with the Strategic Air Command came in full flight uniform bringing his co-pilot (a woman) with him. He explained weather maps from a recent flight over the Rocky Mountains and each student was given a map. After the presentation, the students could try on a parachute he'd brought.

3. A local television weatherman presented a grand finale for a unit on

weather. He showed slides, a hands-on presentation on how to make a rain gauge (coffee can and ruler) and charts of weather in the area. He, too, had weather maps for each child to keep.

4. Following a unit on fish, a man from the Department of Fish and Game discussed the life cycles of various fish in the region. He had slides and charts and each child received a booklet to keep.

WHERE TO FIND SPEAKERS

Here are eight teacher-tested methods for securing outside classroom speakers:

Radio: Talk-show radio attracts speakers, authors and authorities on a variety of subject areas. Whether at home or in a car, keep a pencil and pad nearby. Jot down the names and telephone numbers for people you think might complement your classroom curriculum.

Social Functions: Keep your ears open at parties and as you visit friends. You might hear the name of a speaker you could use. Let your friends know of your upcoming science units.

Government Agencies: Ask for the public affairs officer at your local fire department, fish and game or forest service.

Military Bases: If you live near a military base, call the public affairs office. Military bases often provide speakers as a means of establishing good will between the base and the surrounding community.

Television Stations: Your local TV station has authorities in a variety of areas, including weather. Having children meet a personality they have soon on TV is great public relations for any channel.

Parents and Relatives: Students' family members are often involved in jobs or hobbies which relate to your teaching curriculum. Most parents are honored to be asked to come into the classroom for a presentation.

Other Sources: If you teach near a college campus, call there and ask for their public relations department. Also, local businesses or service clubs like Rotary have a list of speakers. To offer a speaker a larger audience, ask another class to join you.

Telephone Book: If you can't find a speaker for a specific topic by using the seven methods listed, try "walking through the yellow pages" of your telephone book. A call to any number of agencies listed in this useful book can provide names of available resource people in your community.

TWO WEEKS BEFORE YOUR SPEAKER'S VISIT

When asking speakers to come to your classroom, it is important that you follow through after the initial request. Two weeks before the presentation, write to the speaker and thank him or her for agreeing to speak. Send a detailed map showing your school and including the date, time, room and the school telephone number.

Science Speakers

Explain that things which students can touch, see and smell make a speaker's topic come alive in the classroom. Offer suggestions of what to bring.

Here are some examples:

Maps: Many speakers have access to a variety of maps. Not only can they be used in the classroom but students enjoy taking them home and sharing them with their parents.

Booklets: Many agencies and organizations offer booklets as a resource for their presentations. You can also obtain materials for your students (all free) from a number of sources.

Slides/Movies: "A picture is worth a thousand words," we are told. Never is this more true than when pictures are coordinated with the speaker's message. Hearing and seeing slides of a giant beetle on a five-foot screen is most impressive. Visuals carry a powerful message.

TIMELY TIP: **Better yet, as part of a language/penmanship lesson, have your students write for materials to the various agencies in your area.**

ONE WEEK BEFORE YOUR SPEAKER'S VISIT

Build the week's vocabulary and spelling list around words relating to the speaker's topic. The students will feel more comfortable and the speaker will enjoy the give and take with prepared students.

If computers are available to your students, select several lessons which go along with the speaker's topic. One week before the presentation, have the students do the lessons on the computer. The more knowledge they have of the subject the more interested and enthusiastic they will be.

THREE DAYS BEFORE YOUR SPEAKER'S VISIT

Call the speaker. Repeat how much you are looking forward to the visit and review details such as time, place and directions to the school and parking information. Be sure to ask if equipment such as a slide projector or screen might be needed. Don't forget to mention if the speaker must check in at the school office before coming to your room .

PREPARING YOUR STUDENTS

Speakers enjoy walking into rooms where the students have been prepared for their presentation. Plan an art lesson which is coordinated with the visit and be sure your bulletin board carries out the theme. During art have your students design name tags to wear. They should carry a logo for the topic of the day such as a bug, cloud or fish. If you have news clippings about the speaker, be certain they are posted prominently.

THE DAY OF THE VISIT

Have your students draw a welcoming message on your chalkboard and be sure to have an adult-sized chair. You may want to provide refreshments. Be sure to have a glass of water available for your speaker.

If the visitor must check in at the school office, send the Class President to lead the way to the classroom. You may wish to rehearse this ahead of time.

Before the speaker leaves, you may wish to present him or her with a certificate of appreciation— either one your school supplies or one your class has made. For ideas on science resources and how to design awards, see page 142 in Teacher Resources.

Science Speakers

THANK YOU

Within two days after the visit, write your own thank-you note to the speaker. Your students should write personal notes, too. During an art period they might also draw a picture of something which interested them from the presentation. Send the pictures along with the letters.

Speakers enjoy the attention. Many of them spend hours preparing for a single presentation. Let them know how much you appreciate their efforts in providing an outstanding science program for your class.

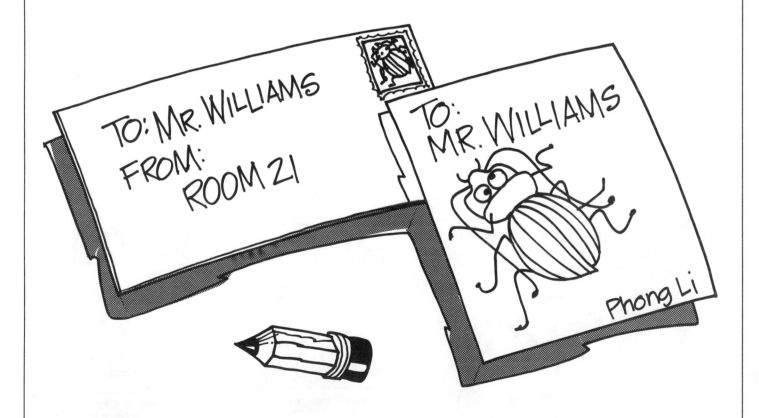

Chapter 20

Music Is Like Oxygen.
Without It — What Is Life?

- Kindergarten Book and Song

- Art Lesson

- First Grade Music Lesson

- Teddy Bear Party

- Music Lessons for Grades Three and Four

- Musical Families

Music Is Like Oxygen. Without It — What Is Life?

Objectives
• To teach singing, movement and rhythm
• To provide enjoyment by using music with literature
• To show students how to memorize a song
• To teach students the history of music

Materials
Books
Drums
Pots, pans and cymbals
Carrot seeds
Carrots
Tea
Paper cups
Toothpicks
Pencils
Paper
Crayons, felt pens
Phonograph
Cassette recorder
Tape
Record
Teddy bears
Map of the United States
Teddy bear-shaped crackers or breakfast cereal

Suggested Ages
Five to ten

Lesson

Music in the classroom provides students with an opportunity to express their feelings, engage in movement and become involved on a different learning level from the basic core subjects.

To provide musical value to your students, devise activities to accompany a children's book. These activities can include movement (rhythm) as well as ethnic dances. In this chapter, three music lessons using children's books will be given.

TIMELY TIP: **If you aren't musical or if you are without music resources, have your music specialist, another teacher or a parent record appropriate songs on tape. Use these tapes to introduce your children to music. If you do not have musical instruments in your classroom, develop a "kitchen" band with pots and pans for instruments and oatmeal boxes for drums.**

KINDERGARTEN BOOK AND SONG

BOOK: _The Carrot Seed_
by Rachel Krauss

Method to introduce the book and song:
Read the book to your students, showing the pictures as you read.
Sing the song about carrots.
Write these words on the chalkboard:
I watered it.
I pulled the weeds.
Yes, carrots grow from carrot seeds.

Ask: Why are we singing? Why is the farmer whistling? Write words on the chalkboard which students do not know.

Bring in a package of carrot seeds and place several seeds in each child's hands. Ask questions such as: Where do we plant seeds? What must we do to make them grow? How long do you think it takes for a carrot to grow to be large enough to eat?

Buy ten carrots with tops at the store. Scrape the skins off and cut into thirds and pass out for students to eat.

Cut off carrot tops so you can "plant" them. Insert toothpicks through the sides of the cups to hold carrots an inch from the top so your students can watch them grow. Fill each cup with water until the water touches the bottom of carrot. Add water every few days.

ART LESSON

Provide students with pencils, crayons and 8 1/2" x 11" paper.

Ask your students to draw their favorite vegetable. The following day, have the children bring their pictures to the "sitting circle." Hold up the pictures and change the word to the song for each one. For example, sing *"Watermelons grow from watermelon seeds,"* or, *"Oranges grow from orange seeds."*

Combine all the pictures into one 8 1/2" x 11" classroom book and write the words on each page. Place the book on a table for students, parents and visitors to read.

FIRST GRADE MUSIC LESSON

BOOK: *The Teddy Bear Book* by Jimmy Kennedy, comes with a record by Bing Crosby.

Read the book aloud to students and show pictures as you read. Play the record as students listen; then teach the chorus of the song.

The Carrot Seed

I watered it I pulled the weeds; carrots grow from car-rot seeds!

Music Is Like Oxygen. Without It — What Is Life?

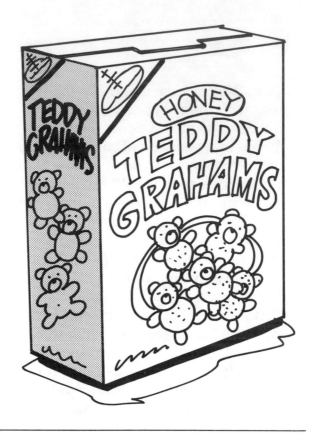

ART LESSON

Write on the chalkboard all glossary words which students need to know and teach these before the art lesson.

Read *The Teddy Bear Book* again, look at the pictures and sing along with the record. Then draw pictures of bears.

Students will need crayons, pencils and 8 1/2" x 11" drawing paper. Tell students to draw a picture of a teddy bear to go into the teddy bear class book.

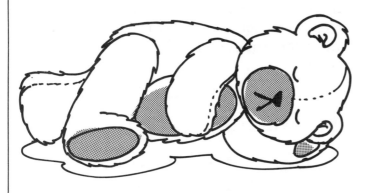

TIMELY TIP: **Use the "Echo Process" for teaching words and music to a song. Teach one line of words at a time and use the rhythm in the song for the words. Go back and teach two lines at a time, then go back and teach four lines at a time. Finally sing the song while holding the book open so students can see pictures as they sing.**

TEDDY BEAR PARTY

Several days before the party, tell students to bring their own teddy bears from home on the day of the party. Since some children may not have teddy bears, tell them they can bring a doll or toy.

The day of the party, bring hot tea and teddy bear-shaped cookies or crackers to school. Explain that students should "serve" their teddy bears tea and grahams before they eat and drink. Then sing the song and read the story again.

On another day, play the record and have students march around the classroom with their kitchen band to the beat of the teddy bear song.

After the parade, read the classroom version of the teddy bear book while the students look at the art work.

MUSIC LESSONS FOR GRADES THREE AND FOUR

BOOK: _Ben's Trumpet_
by Rachel Isador

This is an outstanding book to use all year and especially during Black History month.

Questions to ask: What is a trumpet? Where have you heard a trumpet before? What kinds of music do you hear with a trumpet playing? Some replies might be: In fairy tales, and When the king is coming.

Explain that the trumpet is often used in jazz and ask: What is jazz? Where do you hear jazz?

Have a large map of the United States available. Point out New Orleans and talk about the history of jazz. Ask: What is Dixieland jazz?

Hold up the book and slowly turn the pages, talking about each picture. The setting for the story is in a tenement section of a large city. Ask: Does this book look like a family that might live next door to you? Where would you find this family? Does anyone in your family play an instrument? How many musicians live near you?

Ask: How are these musicians dressed? Why do they wear hats?

Go back and look at the book again. Bring in pictures of a trumpet, oboe, violin and tuba.

Have your students pantomime musical instruments such as a violin, trumpet or trombone.

Music Is Like Oxygen. Without It — What Is Life?

MUSICAL FAMILIES

Using the chalkboard write down categories of musical instruments and their families.

Examples:

Trumpet and trombone—Brass family

Piano and guitar—String family

Saxophone and clarinet—Woodwind family

Drums and cymbals—Percussion family

Explain: In the brass and woodwind families, you blow through an instrument. In the string family, you pluck or bow the strings. In the percussion, you strike the instrument.

ART LESSON

Pass out pencils and 8 1/2" x 11" paper. Before turning on the cassette tape or phonograph, say to your students: I want you to draw what you hear. When you hear fast music, draw fast lines and when you hear slow music, draw slow lines.

Play Dixieland and modern jazz and follow this with an art lesson.

CAUTION: Play the music for only one minute and then stop before students become excited or get wild. Talk about jazz, then play the music again for one minute.

Have students use crayons or felt pens to fill in the loops and circles they have drawn.

To close the unit, read the book one more time. Have students put their names on their artwork and place their pictures on a bulletin board.

For information on ordering these books plus other musical resources, see page 143 in Teacher Resources.

TIMELY TIP: **Do not limit music in your classroom to a few minutes a day. Rather, include music throughout the curriculum as a part of literature, science, math and social studies.**

Chapter 21

Multicultural Activities

- Reducing Cross-Culture Behavior Problems
- Sharing Ideas
- Map and Photo Board Ideas
- Books for Your Classroom Multicultural Library
- All-School Parade
- International Food Day
- Ethnic Cookbooks

Multicultural Activities

Objectives
- To present methods for obtaining Multicultural resources
- To develop a Multicultural calendar
- To increase awareness of other cultures through books, parades and foods

Materials
Computer, software and headphones
Calendar
Large piece of tagboard
Films
Cookbooks
Reading books
World map
Pictures
Flags
Speaker system
Record player and records
Cassette player and tapes

Suggested Ages
Five to twelve

America enjoys an unusually rich and diverse culture. We are a nation of native Americans and millions of immigrants and the influx of newcomers continues every day.

In the past ten years, California alone has seen its population grow by nearly five million people, many from foreign lands.

Similar population explosions have been occurring nationwide. At the same time, in our classrooms during the past decade, we have sought to address the increasing number of minority students.

TIMELY TIP: **Here are two ideas which may help you find tutors for your new foreign students. Your local newspaper may have a column devoted to helping community groups find volunteers. Ask for people who would be willing to work with your students and indicate the native languages of your students. Post messages at local colleges. Adults taking language classes are often willing to work with foreign students to increase their own understanding of the language.**

Here are some ideas for your Multicultural program which can help you now and serve as a resource for you throughout the year. In addition, seek information at your professional library, the Curriculum and Staff Development office and the Multicultural department in your district and by asking minority parents for help.

If you have a computer, have a tutor help new students with language programs. Employ a simple language lesson showing the ABCs, short and long vowels and initial consonants. If possible, have software which uses a headset so the child can hear as well as see the words while working on the computer.

A Multicultural calendar hung prominently on your wall provides both structure and a visible statement of your commitment to studying other cultures.

Divide a large piece of tagboard or construction paper into calendar squares. Prepare one calendar for each month of the school year. On page 146 in Teacher Resources you'll see an example of a calendar. By having each month prepared, you can plan ahead to order films, obtain speakers and prepare for art work to go along with the specific celebrations.

REDUCING CROSS-CULTURE BEHAVIOR PROBLEMS

During the school year, it is important to schedule times when you can discuss "feelings" and "cultural differences" with your students. This can be done during a Class Meeting, a Social Studies period, or spontaneously if problems arise between students during the teaching day.

TIMELY TIP: **If a negative situation arises between two students involving cultural differences either in the classroom or on the playground, it's best to take the two students aside and help them solve the problem right away. In many cases it can be settled quickly and does not need to involve the entire class. You'll need to be the judge of this.**

SHARING IDEAS

If you are a primary teacher, take the opportunity on a holiday, such as Cinco de Mayo, for example, to ask an older student from Mexico to come to your room and share what takes place. Ask questions such as: "What food did you eat yesterday at the celebration?" Or, "Did you celebrate at home or go to a special place?"

SUGGESTIONS: The day before the celebration ask the student to bring samples of the food, artwork or clothes worn at the celebration so your class will not only hear but see how different cultures live.

In the intermediate grades rely on your own students. For instance, you might ask three of your Vietnamese students to form a committee and decide on a class presentation following their return from celebrating their Vietnamese holiday. Meet with them briefly and give them suggestions as to what the students would enjoy seeing, what information would be helpful and provide them with a time frame for the presentation.

You might wish to give them free time, an additional grade in Social Studies or a trip to a fast-food restaurant as a reward following the presentation.

Multicultural Activities

ALL-SCHOOL PARADE

One way to involve the entire school in Multicultural activities is to plan a school-wide parade involving all classrooms and have one committee coordinate the activity. This could be done several ways.

One approach is for all students to celebrate a single event such as the Chinese New Year. Ask students to participate by making Chinese lanterns, a Chinese dragon or masks to wear.

Some teachers might teach their students Chinese songs and dances. Set up a speaker system and phonograph, so students can march around the playground singing and dancing while carrying lanterns or forming a dragon.

Other such parades could be planned to promote cultural understanding by displaying the diversity of your individual students' backgrounds as they wear costumes or carry flags of their ancestors. Still another approach would be to have each classroom study and represent a different culture.

MAP AND PHOTO BOARD IDEAS

You may be able to order a wall world map as a bonus gift through your classroom book club. If not, teacher stores have world maps which can be colored and placed on a wall. Use the map as part of your Multicultural presentation and have your students place pins on towns or villages they or their parents come from.

To further incorporate Multicultural education into your classroom, consider setting aside a bulletin board to use as a photo display of the diverse backgrounds of your students.

You might ask students to bring in pictures showing them at home, at play and at cultural celebrations. The photo board could also display flags and small maps from the various cultures in your room.

TIMELY TIP: **To facilitate the ongoing success of the photo board, establish a "Photo Board Committee." The committee can use your Multicultural calendar to plan special pictures, flags and maps each month.**

BOOKS FOR YOUR CLASSROOM MULTICULTURAL LIBRARY

To increase your students' awareness of the changing world around them, provide them with a variety of Multicultural literature. For a list of books from different cultures, including fables, folktales, picture books, novels and computer software, look at pages 144 and 145 in Teacher Resources.

INTERNATIONAL FOOD DAY

At least once a year set aside a day or week when you feature ethnic foods from many countries. This gives your students an opportunity to celebrate other cultures.

Many cookbooks are now available which feature a country's history, describe the process of bringing foods to the table and provide easy recipes to use in your classroom. For information on seven such books, see page 145 in Teacher Resources.

Notes

Chapter 22

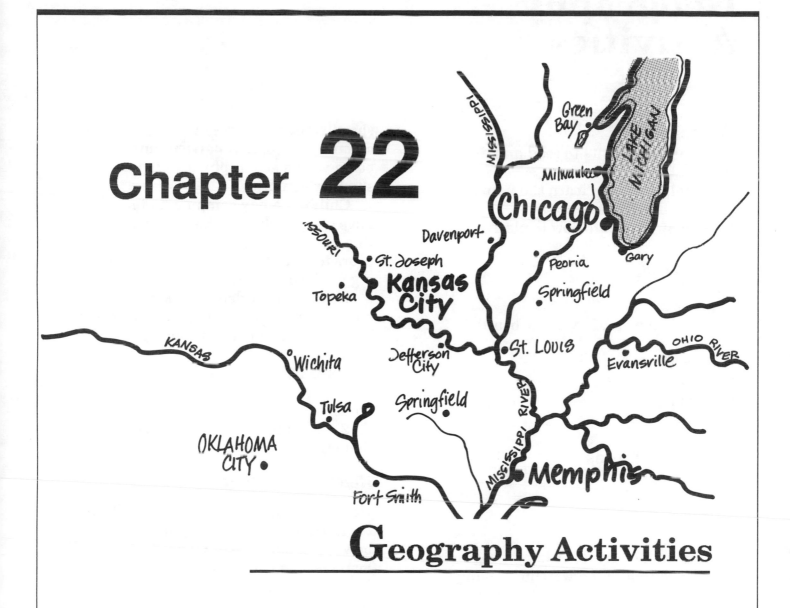

Geography Activities

- Opening-of-School Geography Lesson
- School-Map Project
- Community-Map Unit
- Kindergarten Activities
- Geography Games
- Maps
- Computer Software

Geography Activities

Objectives
• To teach students to read and draw a map
• To help students learn the names of states and capitals
• To show students how to plan a trip

Materials
Paper
Maps
Door or heavy 1 1/2" x 3' x 6' board
Clay
Food coloring
Puzzles
Map games
Computer software

Suggested ages
Five to twelve

Lesson

Students today don't know geography. This is evident when watching young people on television game shows. They simply do not know the names or locations of states, countries or capital cities. Here are some ideas to help you put some pizazz into your geography lessons while teaching geography skills.

OPENING-OF-SCHOOL GEOGRAPHY LESSON

When students return to school after summer vacation, they need interesting, short lessons. One way to make the transition to the regular curriculum is to begin with a geography lesson based upon summer activities.

Children enjoy camping and many will have camped during the summer. Extend this enthusiasm for travel and the out-of-doors to your classroom during the opening weeks of school.

Have your students work alone, with partners or in groups to plan a make-believe trip to a campground in your state.

Here is what you'll need:

1. A road map of your state for each student.

2. Information on the chosen destination from your state park system.

Requirements for the trip

Here is what your students will do:

1. Decide on how long the trip will be, how much money will be needed and how many people will be in each group.

2. Determine the number of miles to the destination and the amount of gasoline needed.

3. Decide on the amount of food to take, number of tents needed and their rental costs and fees for camping sites.

4. Use highlighter felt pens to mark the route from your hometown to the campground.

5. Figure out how much spending money will be needed for extras such as gasoline, snacks, and fees for entry to the campground.

6. Write a detailed log of their day, imagining their activities based upon the literature from the state park office.

Include hand-drawn illustrations or picture post cards depicting the trip.

7. A bulletin board should be set aside for the month the trip is in progress. A member of each group should be assigned to contribute display items such as pictures, maps, a compass, state motto, and picture of state flower and bird.

TIMELY TIP: **For more variety and added learning, have each group pick a different state. Students can send away to the Chamber of Commerce at the state capital to obtain maps, guides and illustrations of parks in the state. The project could be ongoing.**

SCHOOL-MAP PROJECT

This unit can be taught to students from grades two to six. Make it simple for primary grades and more involved for upper-grade students.

Students need to know their own school grounds. With many families moving , students enter school, particularly at the beginning of the year, without any idea of room locations. One way to overcome this is to arrange a unit at the start of the school year which involves students learning about their school while they draw maps.

A leader and a recorder are selected. Other students can perform tasks such as bringing in a compass, maps and drawing materials.

Geography Activities

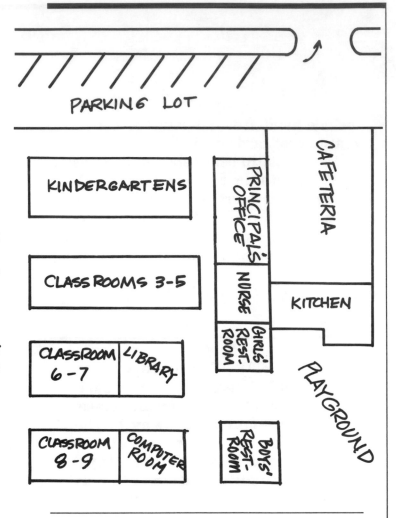

Begin with a walking field trip around the school. Point out classrooms, school office, library, cafeteria, restrooms and kindergarten.

After the tour, have students move around the campus drawing a map of the school. They can sit down on the sidewalk and spread a large sheet of paper out for the map. They should be accurate in their drawings, indicating north, south, east and west and labeling rooms.

Have each student, partners or the group make a formal presentation of their map-drawing experience. Afterward place the maps on the classroom bulletin boards or, if space is not available, above the bulletin boards. Names of all group member should appear on their maps.

HINT: When using a group for the project, it is best to limit the number to four. Each student will have a task and will feel more responsible for doing the work.

TIMELY TIP: **If possible, keep the maps for the spring Open House. Fold them carefully and place in a large drawer until spring. Two weeks before Open House place them on the walls so they will have time to hang out and look neat again.**

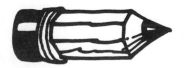

COMMUNITY-MAP UNIT

Once your students have mapped the classroom and the school, move them out to their community.

Purchase a map of your area and enlarge it on a copy machine. Each student should have one copy of the map. Put students into groups based upon the location of their homes. Students living near each other should work together.

HINT: Many maps are copyrighted. Consult your Chamber of Commerce, the visitors' bureau or a county agent for free maps.

To provide an adequate working area when using maps, bring in a large board or door (3' x 6') and place it on sturdy boxes. Cover the board with white paper. Each group will be assigned to work on their area of the map. Only one group should work on the board at a time.

HINT: Draw in the major streets yourself before the students begin. This will provide them with familiar street names as landmarks.

Have students place the following information on the map:
1. Draw in streets.
2. Show all street and traffic lights.
3. Label all streets.
4. Each student will draw his or her house, condo or apartment building and indicate by an "X" on the map where trees, garages, barns or other buildings go in the yard.

The next step is to make clay buildings and trees to place on the map. As an added item of interest, have students color the clay using small amounts of food coloring. Place buildings in position on the map and trees in the yards.

HINT: Warn students ahead of time that they must be very careful when working on the map that they do not damage other houses or trees.

As a culminating activity, take your students on a walking field trip of the community or have them follow the map as they ride their school bus. When going on a walking field trip, have them carry along individual chalkboards, paper and pencils to check out each address and street to verify that the map is correct.

As an oral language assignment, have each group make a presentation on their part of the community. If possible, leave the community board up for Open House. Parents enjoy seeing the community map.

TIMELY TIP: **Place an oilcloth on a table and have students draw an imaginary city with streets, schools, grandma's house, stores, hospitals, railroad tracks and bridges. Younger children will enjoy playing on the map with small cars and trucks.**

Geography Activities

KINDERGARTEN ACTIVITIES

Even five-year-olds need to become acquainted with the world about them. Rubber puzzles of maps of the United States are available in stores and in catalogs. Also, large plastic sheets are available showing the United States so children can walk about and stand on states.

GEOGRAPHY GAMES

Flash cards are available which are brightly colored and indicate a state and show the borders of surrounding states. Not only will students learn names of state, surrounding states and capitals but also the shape of the states.

Take Off ® is a fun game and can be played by kindergartners to adults. It includes a world map, jet planes, flags of nations and a phonetic pronunciation guide for each country.

MAPS

In order to teach geography, it is essential that you have maps in your classroom. Many rooms do not because roller maps are very expensive and many school districts do not have the money to purchase one for each room.

You and your students can make your own by enlarging a small map. Make an overlay map and enlarge it onto butcher paper by using either an opaque or overhead projector. Place the paper on the wall and have students draw in borders, rivers and mountain ranges while labeling major cities and oceans.

For information on geography booklets available from the government, see page 147 in Teacher Resources.

COMPUTER SOFTWARE

Many companies are now featuring computer software to use for teaching geography. Two programs, "Oregon Trail" and "Where In the U.S.A. Is Carmen Sandiego?" are outstanding examples. For information on ordering these programs and others see page 147 in Teacher Resources.

Chapter 23

On the Go
with Field Trips

- Model the Graph
- Day of the Field Trip
- Learning About Towns

On the Go with Field Trips

Objectives
- To become familiar with the world outside the classroom
- To provide a catalyst for students to write about experiences
- To maintain good behavior on field trip

Materials
Cassette player and tape
Graphing paper
Crayons
Pencils
Individual chalkboards
Drinks
Cookies
Sandwich bags

Suggested Ages
Seven to twelve

Lesson

Field trips are important for several reasons. First, they get students out of the classroom and into the real world. Second, they might be the only opportunity for some students to go to a zoo, visit a factory or see a historical site.

As teachers we are asked to have our students do more writing today. A third benefit of field trips is that they provide enjoyable experiences which students need for writing stories. Last, a field trip is a wonderful end-of-the-unit activity for students, bringing alive the things they have been studying and reading about in the classroom.

Some teachers are apprehensive about field trips because of the potential for behavior problems on the bus. If your school has a battery-operated portable microphone, you'll find it invaluable on long trips. Even if you are sitting in the front of the bus, when you use the mike, all the students can hear your instructions clearly. This prevents false information being passed from student to student regarding the assignment and saves your voice as well.

TIMELY TIP: **Check with the customer coordinator where you plan on taking your class before making firm plans. Factories, businesses and parks often have strict age restrictions. Be sure your students are old enough to go on a particular field trip before announcing it to them.**

Another way to promote good behavior is to give each child a project to do on the bus. A good example is a graph such as the one illustrated on page 147. To prepare it, you'll need to drive to the field trip destination dictating into a tape recorder items of interest you pass along the way. Notice, for example, if you see a number of red barns, several churches, or cross many rivers or streams and mark this on the graph.

Before leaving the classroom, it is important to show your students how you want the graph prepared. Explain that they will each have a graph and an individual chalkboard to serve as a desk on the trip as well as a sandwich bag to hold the crayons, pencils and erasers they'll need.

MODEL THE GRAPH

Provide each student with a sample copy of the field-trip graph and make a transparent overlay for your overhead projector by doing the following:

1. Students write their names on their graphs.

2. Read aloud the points of interest at the bottom of the page.

3. Beginning at top right-hand side of graph, read each item and ask students to vote on a color for that item.

4. Students take out chosen crayon and color the square next to, for example, the barn. Continue picking colors and coloring appropriate squares.

5. Go over all colors again and be sure each student understands completely what to do.

6. Explain that students will have partners on the trip and while one looks for barns, the other can color or make an "X" on the square as a reminder to color later.

7. Explain to your students that some columns may have only a few boxes colored while others will have many. For example, they may see only three goats but thirty barns.

DAY OF THE FIELD TRIP

Wait at least 15 minutes before handing out the graphs on the bus so students will have time to settle down and concentrate on what they are to do. Call out the first three objects so all the children are on target and will feel successful before they begin on their own.

TIMELY TIP. **When taking a long field trip, plan for at least one break. Select a rest stop ahead of time with an eye to traffic and restroom facilities. Take along a box filled with cool drinks and a bag of cookies plus some Physical Education equipment. Include a couple of jump ropes which help burn off excess energy in a limited space. After giving your students an opportunity to play and use the restrooms, provide them with a treat before boarding the bus again.**

On the Go with Field Trips

NOTING TOWNS

Prepare students ahead of time for the number of towns you'll be passing through. Tell them you'll alert them as they enter each community so they can look for the name of the town and population sign.

Ask them to write the names and populations of all the towns on the back of their graph. Later, in the classroom discuss the things you've seen such as churches, barns and the towns with largest and smallest populations.

For additional information on field trips, see page 147 in Teacher Resources.

Chapter 24

Rainy-Day Activities

- Nurf® Ball

- Seven Up

- Games Which Teach Math Facts

- Card Games

Rainy-Day Activities

Objective
• To have quiet fun on rainy days

Materials
Board games
Nurf ® ball or Fluff ® ball
Playing cards
Chalkboard, eraser and chalk
Checkers
Dominoes
Cribbage boards

Be prepared from the opening of school for rainy days. Send a note to the parents asking for board games which their children no longer use. Assign one student to go through each game to be sure all parts are there. Place the games in a special drawer or closet which you've labeled, "Rainy-Day Games."

TIMELY TIP: **Assign one student to be the "Gamekeeper." This student can sign the games in and out and also check to be sure all parts are returned. Students understandably get upset when they begin playing a game and find parts are missing.**

NURF® BALL

For a quiet game all your students can play, teach them Nurf ® ball. You can use a Nurf ® ball, a chalkboard eraser or a Fluff ® ball for this game.

Explain that this is a silent game. No talking. All students sit on their desks. One student is designated to begin the game by being the leader. The leader finds a student looking directly at him or her, then throws a ball to that person. If the student drops the ball, he or she must sit down. When eight students are seated, begin the game again.

SEVEN UP

This game is an old standby and one which students enjoy playing year after year. Select seven students to stand in the front of the room. At a signal from a chosen leader, the seated students put their heads down, close their eyes and put one thumb up.

As the seven students walk around the room quietly, each selects one student by touching the student's thumb. The chosen student immediately puts the thumb down to indicate having been chosen and the choosers return to the front of the room.

After seven students have been picked, the leader says, "Heads up." The chosen seven then stand and the leader asks the first person standing to name the student who picked him or her. The game continues until all seven students have had an opportunity to name the persons they think picked them.

If a student guesses correctly, that student walks to the front and the person who picked him or her sits down.

GAMES WHICH TEACH MATH FACTS

Dominoes and cribbage teach basic math facts while providing much pleasure for students. Arrange for several parents who are proficient players to come and work with small groups of students at the beginning of the year. In turn, these students will teach others who may not have played these games.

CARD GAMES

Many students enjoy playing card games on rainy days. Some will bring a deck of their favorite cards from home. Provide a place for them to play either on the floor or on a table.

TIMELY TIP: **The busier you can keep your students during recess and lunch hours on rainy days, the easier it will be on you. Be sure they all go to the bathroom and get a drink when they leave the cafeteria to return to the room. This will cut down on their running outside which can lead to fooling around.**

For additional rainy-day ideas, see page 148 in Teacher Resources.

Notes

Chapter 25

Fund Raisers

- What to Do

- Enlist Parents

- Advertise, Advertise, Advertise

Fund Raisers

Objectives
- To raise money for the classroom
- To advertise classroom sales effectively
- To put on a successful sale

Materials
Cupcakes
Cookies
Sno-Cone ingredients and cups
Popcorn
Tagboard for signs
Felt pens
$10 in change
Cash box
Monthly calendar

If you want your teaching day to be more than simply following the teacher's editions in reading, language and math, you'll probably need to come up with extra money.

No longer can you depend upon your principal, the school board or parents to send you extra money for a field trip, a new set of encyclopedias or even a map for your wall. You'll have to find a way to do this yourself.

One way is to put on at least one BIG sale each year. One teacher conducted two sales and raised $740 to take her class on not one but two outstanding field trips.

WHAT TO DO

Decide what would be easy to sell and bring in the most money. One veteran teacher conducts a sale every October. She sells cupcakes (donated by parents),

cookies (purchased from a bakery at a special price), Sno-Cones and bags of popcorn. She always makes a great deal of money.

ADVERTISE

To make any Fund Raiser work, you must advertise, advertise and do it again. You must get the students excited about your event.

Here are several suggestions: Have your students paint large, colorful signs to advertise the sale. Hang these each morning on walls all around the school. Be sure to take them down at night to protect them from vandals who might deface them or rip them down. Rehang the next day. Have a committee in charge of sign hanging.

Either you or your students can make a sandwich board out of two large pieces of tagboard for *you* to wear. The sign should be colorful, illustrate each item to be sold and list the prices beside each sweet treat.

You should then prepare your class to go out with you for the entire week before the sale. Teach them words such as *"Friday, on Friday, cupcakes on Friday... Hip, Hip Hooray, Yum, Yum."* Use the tune from *Annie* called, "Tomorrow, Tomorrow."

Before school, during recess and during lunch break, have at least ten of your students walk with you around the school and sing the song. You'll soon find another forty students will want to follow and join in the singing. It makes for great advertising, gets your message across and it's all free!

Ask a parent early to bake at least a dozen *gorgeous* cupcakes for the day before the sale. These should be loaded with frosting and tempting toppings. Now, you walk with your troop and sing your song as you display the enticing cupcakes. You'll find students begging to buy them on the spot. But don't let them. This is your advertising day.

You might also send a brief note to all parents (not just your own students') a few days before your sale. Let them know what you'll be selling and the prices because students will often bring enough money to buy one of everything.

TIMELY TIP: **Be sure you or a dependable parent has all the details worked out for the sale. Let parents know when the cupcakes should arrive. Have a parent bring the popcorn and another pick up the ice for the Sno-Cones. Have all bases covered. Have $10.00 in change and, if possible, have a cash box to keep the coins safe.**

TIMELY TIP: **Check with the bus drivers to be sure they will let students on the bus with food. If not, provide plastic sandwich bags to hold food going home. Drivers appreciate this.**

Use your imagination to come up with other methods for making money. You can sell pencils, popsicles and all sorts of baked goods.

Fund Raisers

TIMELY TIP: At some schools many teachers are eager to make money and you'll need a schedule to be sure you're not selling on the same day. This can be done by making up a large monthly calendar titled, "Bake Sales," and place on the faculty room wall. Ask all teachers to sign up for the days they want. If you have sales too close together, you won't make as much money.

BAKE SALE RM.7

POPCORN SALE RM 9

ICE CREAM RM 3

APRIL — BAKE SALES

S	M	T	W	T	F	S
		1	2	3	4	5 SALE RM.7 6
7	8	9	10 SALE RM 3	11	12	13
14	15	16	17	18	19	20
21	22	23	24	25 SALE RM.9	26	27
28	29	30				

Chapter 26

Reducing Teacher Stress

- Teachers as Decision Makers
- Fourteen Ways to Reduce Stress in Your Life
- The Three "Cs" to Control Teacher Stress
- Ten Brief Ways to a Happier Life

Reducing Teacher Stress

Objective
• To help teachers find ways to reduce stress in their lives

TEACHERS AS DECISION MAKERS

Teachers make 500 decisions *an hour*, second only to air traffic controllers. Their nonstop lifestyle leaves little time for breaks. Recess means yard duty, lunch often means cafeteria monitoring, and the end of the day calls for school bus duty. No wonder we are frazzled, exhausted and short-tempered by the weekend.

"Stress also comes from pushing information day in and day out," says Sue Miller-Hurst, education consultant. "You need ways to get out of this mold."

If you expect to stay in the profession for a lifetime, you must reduce this daily bombardment of stress upon your mind, body and soul.

TIMELY TIP: **One way to reduce stress is to be sure your car will start at the end of the day. Here is a simple tip. When leaving home in fog, rain or darkness in the morning, attach a clothes pin to your ignition key when you turn on your headlights. That way when you arrive at school, you'll remember to turn off your lights.**

FOURTEEN WAYS TO REDUCE STRESS IN YOUR LIFE

Meditation: Before leaving for school each morning, set aside at least 15 minutes for quiet meditation. You may choose a favorite chair and look at a peaceful scene, favorite picture or a pretty flower. You might prefer to simply close your eyes. Allow your mind to relax. Let go of all the things you need to do that day. Instead, be at peace with yourself.

Music: Choose tapes and CDs which offer you periods of peacefulness. If you drive to work, play one in your car. You'll arrive at school much more ready to begin your day.

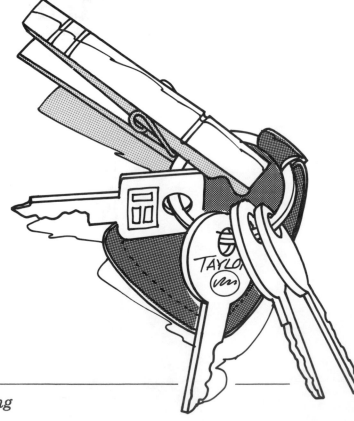

Relaxation and stress workbooks:
More and more books are being written to
help people deal with the hectic pace of
our daily lives. Look on page 148 of
Teacher Resources for the names of excellent books and tapes.

Taking time each day to read a few
paragraphs from such a book can make a
big difference in your life.

Exercise daily: Exercise *vigorously*
for twenty minutes at least three times a
week. You need to get *out* of your mind
and *into* your body each day. You can do
this by taking a daily walk, swimming,
playing tennis, or attending an aerobics
class on a regular basis.

Eat wisely: Have a nutritious breakfast, low in fats and sugars and high in
complex carbohydrates every day. If your
school doesn't offer good lunches, take
your own.

Dance: Dance is the rhythm of the
soul. Use music and movement as a way
to change your way of thinking. You
might enjoy being part of a dance group
or just dancing alone at home to music
you like.

Attitude: Have you checked your
attitude lately? Like oil, our attitude is
what keeps us running smoothly. Have
you lost hope? Begin a daily program to
change your mental patterns. Write down
your blessings and dump your negative
thoughts.

Humor: Plan for ways to put more
humor into your life. Find funny people.
Remember funny jokes. Rent a comedy
video. Don't hang around with people who
criticize all the time.

Naps: One of the best gifts you can
give yourself upon returning home is to
take a twenty-minute nap before beginning your other activities. This will revi-
talize your body and soul.

Affirmations: Find a book on how to
write affirmations. Look in Teacher Resources, page 148, for ideas. Begin to
write these several times each week. Post
one or two on your bathroom mirror.

Think about your students: Change
your way of thinking about your class.
Look into your students' eyes. See them
for the beautiful children they are and
can be.

Run away from home: Plan for a
weekend away from home every two
months if possible. Find a quiet motel
where you can read, think positive

Reducing Teacher Stress

thoughts and get away from home, telephone and television. Be alone.

Monthly massage: Due to the increased stress in our lives, many upscale beauty salons are now incorporating massage into their schedules. Find a good one in your area. Many will suggest you come in thirty minutes ahead of time to relax in the spa before going in for the massage. The hour spent with waterfall music playing in the background as you have every part of your body massaged from your earlobes to your toes does wonders for your body, soul and spirit.

Find a spiritual power in your life: Give yourself the freedom to no longer be "The general manager of the universe." This alone will give you added peace. Give yourself in and up to a higher power. You cannot do it all.

THE THREE "Cs" TO CONTROL TEACHER STRESS

Outstanding writer Dorothy Jongeward says, "To control stress in your life you must:

1. Feel you are in control of the situation. If you do not feel this way, you'll be under more stress.

2. Have a commitment to your job. Especially in teaching which requires so much stamina, you must be dedicated to what you are doing. You must feel you are making a difference in childrens' lives.

3. See your job as a challenge. It might not be perfect, but you must know and understand that you are capable of doing the best job you can."

TEN BRIEF WAYS TO A HAPPIER LIFE

- Be yourself.
- Be kind to yourself.
- Simplify your life.
- Put balance into your life.
- Plan ahead for pleasure.
- Get rid of clutter in your life.
- When you start something new, drop something old.
- Break down big jobs into small pieces.
- Enjoy what you do.
- Be gentle to your mind, your body and your heart.

Teacher Resources

Teacher Resources

CHAPTER 1

Writing Ideas

A yearly booklet with tried and true ideas plus some experiments with writing in the classroom.

Ask for "Teacher Tips," with Back-to-School and writing tips for all disciplines.
Send to:
American Federation of Teachers
555 New Jersey Avenue NW
Washington, DC 20001

Art Ideas

From the Hands of a Child
by Anthony Flores
Order from:
Fearon Teacher Aids
P.O. Box 280
Carthage, IL 62321
Telephone: (916) 351-1912

CHAPTER 2

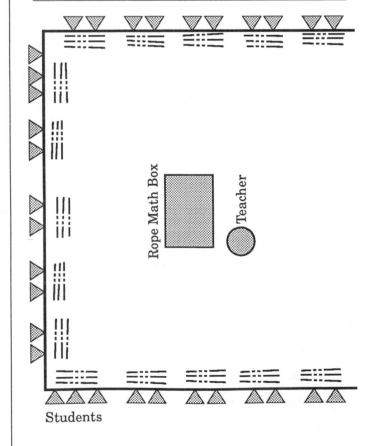

Students

For good math ideas send a #10 self-addressed and stamped envelope to:
National Council of
Teachers of Mathematics
1906 Association Drive
Reston, VA 22091
Telephone: (703) 620-9840

You'll receive an array of information such as math games, puzzles and ideas for helping your students overcome difficulties with math. You can also request that your name be placed on their mailing list for additional materials.

CHAPTER 3

How to Organize and Run a Successful Classroom
by Bonnie Williamson
Order from:
Dynamic Teaching Company
P.O. Box 276711
Sacramento, CA 95827
Telephone: (916) 351-1912

CHAPTER 5

For information on computer software for writing lesson plans *write to*:
National School Products
101 East Broadway
Maryville, TN 37801
Telephone (800) 627-9393

Here are sample shapes for arranging desks by the A-B-C method.

CHAPTER 6

Teacher Resources

CHAPTER 7

A HOME STORAGE IDEA FOR TEACHERS

Teachers are collectors. They must be in order to have sufficient supplies to run a successful classroom. However, the question arises, *"What can I do with all this stuff?"*

Here is what I did. My husband built a storage unit for me in our garage. Since I had taught grades K to 6, I had materials from all these grades which I wanted to keep in case I taught those grades again.

Here is how to build a unit:

1. Decide how many units (boxes) you'll need. Boxes can be cardboard or you can purchase colorful ones with lids from discount stores. I purchased 25 and the illustration indicates this. You can build a smaller unit, if needed.

2. Determine where you'll build the unit. The best place is on one wall of the garage. It could also be built in a basement.

3. Build the frame. See the illustration for amounts of lumber and nails to purchase.

4. After the frame is built, decide on how you'll fill the boxes. For teachers, depending upon the amount of materials you have, set aside as many boxes for each grade level as you'll need.

5. Number each box. Place a 2" x 2" square of colorful plastic tape on the lower right corner of each box. Take a large black felt pen and number each box.

6. Decide ahead of time what you'll place in the high top boxes. Select items you seldom need so you won't be climbing up a ladder often. The most used items should be placed in boxes at eye level.

7. To make the system flow, purchase a small metal file box to keep in the house. Place 3" x 5" cards inside the box with each card indicating the number of the corresponding box in the garage.

8. As you place items in each box, list these items on the card. For example, the contents of box number one are all listed on the index card number one in the card file.

9. Keep the card file in your kitchen or office. Each year update the card file as you toss out or add items to the boxes.

The storage system saves me countless minutes all during the year. Whenever I need something quickly, I look in the card file and find the box number. I immediately go into the garage and retrieve a good read-aloud book, a ditto I need for geography or a record to use during music that day.

How to build the storage unit:

A frame containing 25 boxes will fit on one side of an average two car garage. Begin by purchasing one of the boxes to use as a sizing model. Then purchase the rack materials from a lumberyard. Best buys today can be found by using clear fir to build the frame. Caution: Purchase wood without knots. A great deal of weight can accumulate in boxes, so sturdy wood is essential.

To build a rack for 25 boxes (27"x 16"x 13") five boxes high and five boxes across, buy approximately 48 feet of 2"x 2" clear fir, and 216 feet of 1"x 2" clear fir.

The front of the rack uses six 96" lengths of 2"x 2" fir as upright posts. The remainder of the rack, including the six back upright posts and all other materials for horizontal members, are cut from 1/2" fir. See sketch.

When completed, number the boxes consecutively and fill them. Number the index cards in order. List contents of each box on a single card.

Place the cards in a file box and keep it in a handy place inside the house. There you are. Happy organizing!

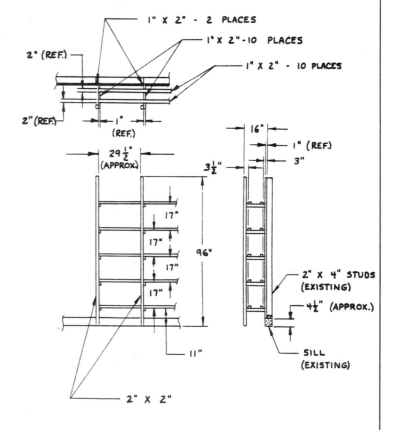

CHAPTER 8

This is a sample of a letter to send home asking for help in the classroom.

George Washington Elementary School
105 Bridge Street
Springfield

September 4, 199__

Dear Families, Grandparents and Friends,

    We want this to be the best year ever for our students. During the school year I'm going to need your help in the classroom. Please look over this page and check where you can help.

Work in the classroom

	8:30-9:30	9:30-10:30	10:30-12:00
___ Monday	_____	_____	_____
___ Tuesday	_____	_____	_____
___ Wednesday	_____	_____	_____
___ Thursday	_____	_____	_____
___ Friday	_____	_____	_____

___ I can grade papers at home at night or on weekends.
___ I can go on field trips with the class.
___ I can do bulletin boards for you.
___ I can help with your physical education program.
___ I can be a class speaker for you. I could speak on this topic: _____
___ I have a hobby or skill which might be of interest to your students.
It is:_____

    Thank you for your help. Please check and return this letter to school by next Friday. I will call and confirm the day and time you'll come to school.

Most sincerely,

Mr. Todd Edward
Teacher, Fourth grade

Teacher Resources

CHAPTER 9

TIPS ON HOW TO END THE YEAR AND CLOSE YOUR CLASSROOM WITHOUT LOSING YOUR MIND

1. Don't put things away too early. If you do, your students will begin to misbehave.

2. During the last ten days of school, present short lessons followed by art and craft projects and Physical Education.

3. Be sure your students have returned all library books.

4. If you have animals in the classroom, arrange well in advance to have students take them home for the summer.

When moving to another classroom:

If you must move, bring in a wheelbarrow or wagon. Carefully label your boxes, then have two dependable students take them to the new room. Be sure they know exactly where you wish to put the boxes.

Cleaning your classroom:

Here is what you'll need for the final week of school:

1. A large jug of spray cleaner
2. Ten to twenty sponges
3. At least three or four small pails for water
4. Several clean rags for dusting
5. A cleanser like Comet®

Assign each of your students a partner to help clean the classroom. Type a ditto listing all jobs to be done and assign students to each job or let them choose what they want to do. Go over the ditto aloud in the classroom, then have students put their names where they will work. For example, if John and Ramon will be cleaning two shelves of the classroom library, they should post their names on these shelves.

Here are examples of jobs for students:

1. Collect all rulers and clean them with a sponge and spray cleaner. Once they are dry, store in the drawer which says "rulers."

2. Clean out two bookshelves. Remove books and wipe shelf with a sponge and spray cleaner. All books must be dusted and then placed back on the shelves. Use masking tape to put students' names on assigned shelves and cupboards. For fun, I also bring white gloves the final day to check. The students will work very hard to pass the "glove test."

3. Clean all scissors and put in the sun to dry (leave them open while drying). Place in a drawer labeled "scissors."

4. Remove all materials from under the sink. Clean, wipe, dry and dust and replace them in neat order.

5. Take down bulletin boards and place in labeled envelopes.

6. Take down the flag.

7. Clean all Physical Education equipment.

8. Enclose all your open shelves with paper for the summer if your school requires it.

All students should do the following:

1. Erase all marks from all their books.

2. Repair all ripped pages with clear tape.

NOTE: Assign one dependable student from each station to be sure this is done.

3. After all books have been turned in, each student must take a sponge and spray cleaner and clean both the inside and outside of his/her desk and chair.

CAUTION: I've had to stay to clean out desks abandoned by students. Don't let this happen to you.

4. If you have two students you can trust, have them clean out your desk. Many students enjoy sorting out paper clips, rubber bands, pencils and all the rest and then cleaning out the drawers.

Summer school classroom:

If your room will be used by another teacher and class for summer school, you need to plan ahead for storage. If you have personal items, assign a student to deliver them to your car to take home.

The remaining items are more secure if you place them in a closet and lock them up for the summer.

Vandalism:

More and more schools are being vandalized during the summer months when few people are around. You need to prepare for this. Check with your principal regarding proper storage of all school equipment such as VCRs, televisions, computers and overhead projectors. It is not wise to have students carry or push expensive pieces of equipment around the school. Instead, ask the custodian to remove special equipment and lock it up for you.

Payoff for your students:

Alert your students ahead of time that you expect them to behave and do their best job cleaning the room. If they do, let them know you will do one of the following (or add one of your own):

1. Take them to a nearby park for a picnic.
2. Buy pizza and bring to the classroom one day.
3. Take them to a nearby pool for a swimming party.

HINT: When you go swimming, have permission slips from all parents so you are covered in case of an accident and have plenty of parents to help.

For you to do:
1. Before leaving school, be sure your register is completed and all inked.
2. Ask your principal if you should push all desks to one corner of the room before you leave.
3. When you finish, turn in your key and go out for a special treat to celebrate the end of a year!

Classroom Stamps

For a booklet on outstanding stamps for classroom use *order from:*
        Fearless Design
        P.O. Box 8487
        Santa Cruz, CA 95061
        Telephone: (408) 423-9340

CHAPTER 11

Writing Grants for Computers

1. Ask for informational help from your local school district or state Department of Education Office. Ask for Special Projects or Technology division.

2. An outstanding book is Foundation Center's User Friendly Guide: A Grant Seeker's Guide To Resources. Some libraries have this book but not all.

3. To locate your nearest Foundation Center, call (212) 620-4230 or write Foundation Center, Eighth Floor, 79 Fifth Avenue, New York, NY 10003.

Sources for Computer Software

        Publishers of Weekly Reader Software
        Optimum Resource, Inc.
        10 Station Place
        Norfolk, CT 06058
Includes such programs as: *Stickybear Math* and *Stickybear Reading.*

•

        Springboard Software, Inc.
        7808 Creekridge Circle
        Minneapolis, MN 55435
Includes software on how to produce a newsletter with graphics.

•

        Beagle Bros., Inc.
        6215 Ferris Square, Suite 100
        San Diego, CA 92121
This company has an Apple II software catalog including Applesoft Games, software for drawing pictures and graphs and much more.

•

        Davidson and Associates, Inc.
        3135 Kashiwa Street
        Torrance, CA 90505
This company produces Word Attack software in English, Spanish and French in addition to a reading and language arts program. Their *Math Blaster* and *Spell It Plus* have been well received in classrooms.

•

        Broderbund Software
        Carmen Series
        Education Software Services
        40 San Domingo Way
        Novato, CA 94945
This company produces excellent software on critical thinking skills and geography.

•

        Orange Cherry Talking Schoolhouse
          Software
        P.O. Box 390
        Pound Ridge, NY 10576
This company produces software for Apple 11GS, IBM and Tandy. Software ranges from problem-solving skills to foreign languages.

When purchasing this software, the customer may sign a contract allowing him or her to copy the software for a specific added price. Call (800) 672-6002 for more detailed information.

CHAPTER 12

Awesome Elementary School Physical Education Activities by Cliff Carnes
Order from:
        Dynamic Teaching Co.
        P.O. Box 276711
        Sacramento, CA 95827
        Telephone: (916) 351-1912

Teacher Resources

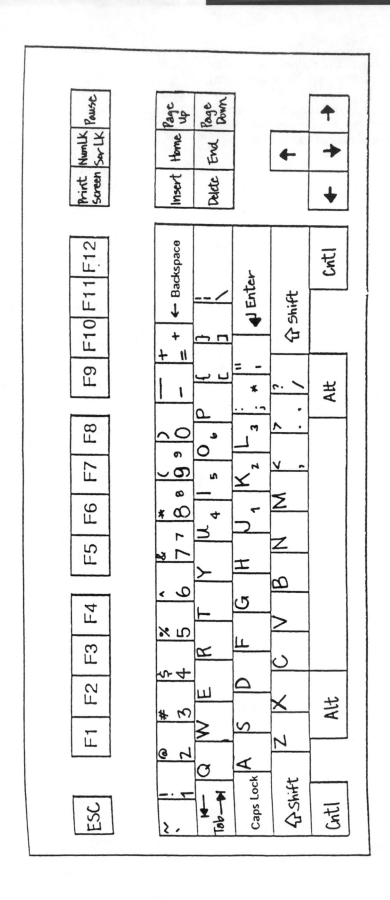

CHAPTER 13

Name_____ Date _____

My partner is _____

MERRY MEASUREMENT - PART I

Station One: Weight Station
1. Estimate and record your partner's weight in pounds. _____.
    Weigh your partner. How much in pounds _____? How many ounces would this be? _____.

Station Two: Canned-Food Station
1. How much do you estimate the tuna can weighs in ounces? _____. How much *does* it weigh? _____.
    How much would two cans weigh? _____ounces.
2. How much do you think the soup can weighs in ounces? _____. How much *does* it weigh? _____. How much would three cans weigh? _____.

Station Three: Food-Weighing Table
You may eat up to six ounces of fruit, but you may not eat all of one kind. You must cut at least one slice of each.

Station Four: Estimation Station
1. Estimate the weight of the potato. _____ ounces. Weigh the potato. _____ ounces.
2. Guess how many paper clips are in the bowl. _____. Place them on the plastic lid to weigh.
    How much do they all weigh? _____ ounces.
3. Guess how many beans are in the bowl. _____. Place them on the plastic lid. How much do they weigh? _____ounces.
The class will count the paper clips and beans tomorrow.

Station Five: Jar Station
1. Fill the measuring cup with water. How many ounces in a cup? Read from the cup. _____ounces.
2. Use the measuring cup to fill the pint jar. How many ounces in a pint? _____.
3. Use the measuring cup to fill the quart jar. How many ounces in a quart? _____.

Station Six: Fun Money Station

HAVE FUN WITH YOUR NAME!
Write out your full name on a piece of paper. Find out how much your name is worth.
Use the code below.
a, e, i, o, u = 5 cents each
b, c, g, j, k, l, n, p, s, t, v = 4 cents each
d, f, h, m, r, w = 6 cents each
q, x, y, z = 10 cents each

My name is _____.

My name is worth _____.

My partner's name is worth _____.

KEEP THIS PAPER IN YOUR MATH BOOK UNTIL TOMORROW.
WE WILL DISCUSS ALL ANSWERS AT THAT TIME.

Teacher Resources

CHAPTER 15

TO RETAIN OR NOT TO RETAIN, THAT IS THE QUESTION

If retention is a possibility

If there is even a *possibility* of retention, the parents should be told at the Fall parent conference. You *cannot* wait until May.

Why retain?

If a child is small or emotionally immature, or has completed kindergarten or first grade and is still lacking the necessary academic survival skills, retention should be considered.

TIMELY TIP: **Before retaining a student be sure you've sought out all avenues of help such as school counselor, psychologist and nurse. A complete battery of tests should be given to verify the child is in good emotional, physical and mental health.**

Why *not* retain?

Many studies about the effectiveness of retaining students have been conducted in recent years and the consensus of opinion is not to retain.

Studies reveal that in grades one to five, retention helps only one out of three students and that while retained students do make progress during the year they repeat a grade, it isn't as much as similar children who are promoted. Contrary to popular belief, the average negative effect of retention on *achievement* is even greater than the negative effect on emotional adjustment and self-concept.

A chance to avoid retention

Offer the parents two options, 1) retain the student, or 2) have the parents and child sign a contract promising additional, specialized help over the summer. This means summer school or hiring a tutor to work with the student.

The contract should include a statement from you addressing subject areas, skills and major deficiencies. Also, specify that a report must come from the summer school teacher or tutor as to number of days spent with the child, work covered and progress made.

Explain that the child will be given a test in September on the material studied to be sure he or she is ready for the next grade. In this way, the decision is left up to the parents and the student. For a sample contract which you may copy, see the next page.

NOTE: Check to find out your district's policy on retaining a student due to limited English. In many states, a student may not be retained for this reason.

When a student is retained

If you do retain a student, you need to have a very definite individual academic plan in September to ensure that he or she will receive instruction geared to the areas of greatest need. Consider keeping the student in your classroom since you know his or her ability and personality patterns.

George Washington Elementary School

PARENT, STUDENT AND TEACHER SUMMER CONTRACT
June _____

In lieu of retention, I will seek educational help during the summer for my child,

_____
Name of Student

Check one   Summer School _____   Tutoring _____

═══

Teacher to complete the following:

Grade level _____
Circle area(s) of needed improvement: Reading, Language, Math or _____.

1. Subject _____

   Skills needed: _____

   _____

   _____

2. Subject _____

   Skills needed: _____

   _____

   _____

Parent completes the following:

I, _____, will enroll my child in (circle one) summer school or tutoring program in
Name of Parent/Guardian
the areas noted by the teacher. I fully understand that my child must attend summer school or be tutored to go
on to the next grade in September. I also understand that my child must pass a test the first week of school in
September to move to the next grade. I will submit a copy of this form to the summer school/tutor and will return
the form at the bottom of this page to George Washington School in the Fall.

_____   _____
Parent Signature   Student Signature

_____   _____
Teacher Signature   Date

TO BE RETURNED TO GEORGE WASHINGTON SCHOOL IN SEPTEMBER
- -

_____ attended summer school, or was tutored, at _____
Student's name   Name of school
from _____ to _____. He/she missed _____ days during the program. I feel this child is
Date   Date
ready/not ready to move on to the next grade.

_____   _____
Name of Teacher/Tutor   Telephone Number

Teacher Resources

Self-Esteem

A Classroom Calendar
by Maria Turner
This 35-week lesson planner uses five components for building self-esteem in the classroom. It focuses on security, self-concept, belonging, purpose, and competence.
Order from:
Educational and Training Services
P.O. Box 1532
Santa Cruz, CA 95061
Telephone: (408) 426-6850

Self-Esteem
by Virginia Satir
see above address

Songs of Self-Esteem
by Minnie O'Leary
see above address

Awards, Rewards and Marvelous Messages
by Anthony Flores
Order from:
Fearon Teacher Aids
P.O. Box 280
Carthage, IL 62321
Telephone: (800) 242-7272

Building Self-Esteem in Children
by Patricia Beme
Continuum Publishing Company
New York

Raising Positive Kids in a Negative World
by Zig Ziglar
Thomas Nelson Press
Nashville, TN

CHAPTER 16

How to Organize and Run a Successful Classroom, chapters five and seven
by Bonnie Williamson
Order from:
Dynamic Teaching Co.
P.O. Box 276711
Sacramento, CA 95827
Telephone: (916) 351-1912

CHAPTER 19

For ideas on how to make Award Certificates *write to:*
Fearon Teacher Aids
P.O. Box 280
Carthage, IL 62321
Ask for: Awards, Rewards and Marvelous Messages by Anthony Flores

Science Books as Resources

Sharks in Action
Early-Reader Pop-ups
Aladden Books
Macmillan Publishing Co.
866 Third Avenue
New York, NY 10022

The Bug Book
by Dr. Hugh Danks
Workman Publishing Co.
708 Broadway
New York, NY 10003
Describes the appearance and behavior of twenty-six common insects and other creepy crawlies, including the grasshopper, ant and centipede, with simple instructions on catching, keeping and studying them.

Gravity Is a Mystery
The Sun: Our Nearest Star
What the Moon Is Like
Order from:
Harper & Row Junior Books
10 East 53rd Street
New York, NY 10022

Backyard Scientist
by Jane Hoffman
Order from:
Dynamic Teaching Company
P.O. Box 276711
Sacramento, CA 95827
Telephone: (916) 351-1912
A book with twenty-five experiments that kids can perform using things found around the house. Ages 4 to 12.

CHAPTER 20

Books To Use With Music

The Carrot Seed
by Rachel Isadora
Order from:
    Harper and Row
    10 E. 53rd St.
    New York, NY 10022

The Teddy Bears' Picnic
by Jimmy Kennedy
Order from:
    Green Tiger Press
    435 E. Carmel Street
    San Marcos, CA 92069
    Telephone: (800) 424-2443

Ben's Trumpet
by Rachel Isadora
Order from:
    Greenwillow Books
    William Morrow and Company
    105 Madison Ave.
    New York, NY 10016

Additional Resources for your Music Library

Ready-to-Use Music Activities Kit
by Audrey J. Adair
    Park Publishing Company
    West Nyack, NY
Over 200 fun-filled classroom activities to build basic skills in music theory, singing, composing, listening, ear training and instruments of the band and orchestra. All in student worksheet form ready for immediate duplication and use.

The Second Raffi Songbook
by Catherine Ambrose
    Crown Publishers, Inc.
    New York, NY
Forty-two songs from Raffi's albums *Baby Beluga, Rise and Shine* and *One Light, One Sun.*

Let's Begin with a Song
by Doris Edmund
    Creative Teaching Press, Inc.
    Monterey Park, CA
Songs and learning activities for K-2.

Sail Away
Selected and edited by Eleanor G. Locke
Order from:
    Boosey and Hawkes, Inc.
    52 Cooper Square - Tenth Floor
    New York, NY 10001
    Telephone: (800) 645-9582
155 American Folk Songs to sing, read and play.

Tapes, Filmstrips and Prints on Jazz

"New Orleans - Birth of Jazz"
"Chicago - Golden Age of Jazz"
"The Years When Swing Was King"
"From Be-bop Till Today"
"Listening to Jazz"
An excellent introduction for music appreciation courses. See below for ordering.

Popular Music Study Prints
One hundred prints (11"x14") featuring famous jazz personalities and marching bands from early jazz to the Age of Rock.
Order from:
    Educational Audio-Visual Inc.
    Pleasantville, NY 10570
           •

Meet the Instruments
This collection includes posters, study prints, filmstrips and recordings to explore the sights and sounds of the symphony orchestra and band.
           •

Primary Rhythms
A collection of taped recordings designed to develop the joy of rhythmic response through music.
"Fun with Music"
"The Rainy Day Record"
"Holiday Rhythms"
Order from:
    Belwin Mills Publishing Corporation
    Melville, NY 11747

"On the Move"
by Greg and Steve
Two outstanding tapes: "Rock to the Music" and "Scat Like That"
Order from:
    Youngheart Records
    P.O. Box 27784
    Los Angeles, CA 90027

Teacher Resources

The following publishers offer free catalogs of their books or computer software.

Reading Books

Sundance Publishers
P.O. Box 1326
Littleton, MA 01460
Telephone: (800) 456-5584

Reading Books and Cookbooks

Lerner Publications
241 First Avenue North
Minneapolis, MN 55401
Telephone: (800) 328-4929

Resource Books with Information on Students Arriving from Other Countries

The Hmong: Yesterday and Today
Iu Mien: Tradition and Change
by Pat Moore-Howard
Order from:
2731 Sutterville Road
Sacramento, CA 95820
Telephone: (916) 451-2477

Two outstanding books written by a mentor teacher who has travelled to the Far East to study these two cultures. A *MUST READ* resource for all teachers working with children from these countries.

Computer Software

Orange Cherry Talking Software
P.O. Box 390
Pound Ridge, NY 10576
Telephone: (800) 672-6002

National School Products
101 East Broadway
Maryville, TN 37801
Telephone: (800) 627-9393

EISI
2225 Grant Road
Los Altos, CA 94024
Telephone: (800) 955-5570

Multicultural Literature

Author	Book Title	Grades	Country or Culture
Musgrove	Ashanti to Zulu: African	K-1	Africa
Carpenter	Tales of a Korean Grandmother	K-2	Korea
Wolkstein	The Banza	K-3	Black
Anonymous	Grandfather's Stories	K-3	Philippines
Cooney	Tortillas Para Mama	K-3	Mexico
Lewin	Jafta: The Journey	K-3	South Africa
Knutson	How the Guinea Fowl Got Her Spots	K-3	Africa
Pittman	The Gift of the Willows	K-4	Japan
Stelson	Safari	K-4	Africa
Gustafson	The Hero of Barletta	K-4	Italy
Scott	Egyptian Boats	K-4	Egypt
Haskins	Count Your Way Through Russia	1-4	Russia
Hodges	The Wave	1-4	Japan
Souci	The Legend of Scarface: A Blackfeet Indian Tale	2-3	Native American
St. John	A Family in Hungary	2-5	Hungary
Keats	John Henry: An American Legend	2-5	Black American
Dutton	An Arab Family	2-5	Oman
Taylor	A Kibbutz in Israel	2-5	Israel
Bennett	A Family from Brazil	2-5	Brazil
Reiff	The Family from Vietnam	3-6	Vietnam
Hien	Doi Song Moi: A New Life in a New Land	3-6	Vietnam
Harkonen	The Children of China	3-6	China
Harkonen	The Children of Egypt	3-6	Egypt
Louie	Yeh-Shen: A Cinderella Story from China	3-6	China
Luenn	The Dragon Kite	3-6	Japan
Goble	The Girl That Loved Wild Horses	4-8	Native American
Casagrand & Johnson	Focus on Mexico	5-8	Mexico
Hamilton	The People Could Fly	6-8	China

Ethnic Food Cookbooks

Holiday Cooking Around the World
Edited by Philip E. Baruth

Teachers searching for a unique way to celebrate various international holidays will appreciate this collection of ethnic recipes from fifteen countries. Each section begins with an introduction of the geography, culture and types of foods of each country.

Some books focus on a single region.
Suggested ages - Five through high school

Author	Book Title
Nabwire & Montgomery	Cooking the African Way
Yu	Cooking the Chinese Way
Weston	Cooking the Japanese Way
Coronado	Cooking the Mexican Way
Plotkin	Cooking the Russian Way
Nguyen & Monroe	Cooking the Vietnamese Way

Teacher Resources

A SAMPLE OF MULTICULTURAL CELEBRATIONS FOR SEPTEMBER

September

2. The Democratic Republic of Vietnam was established in 1945.
3. A celebration of the Akan people's journey to settle near water in North Ghana — The Akwambo Festival
4. The Sunrise Dance is held by the Apache Indians to celebrate the 14th birthday of White Mountain Girls.
7. In the United States and Canada workers are honored on Labor Day.
8. This is International Literacy Day.
9. Jewish New Year begins — Rosh Hashanah
10. The Chinese celebrate their good harvest — Moon Festival
15. International Day of Peace
16. The New Year, Muharram, is celebrated by people of Islam.
17. This is Citizenship Day for Libyan Arab Jamshirtha.
18. The Jewish Holy Day, Yom Kuppur
20. Children's Day in Germany
21. Thanksgiving Day in the Philippines
22. Spring begins in the Southern Hemisphere.
23. The Jewish Thanksgiving, Sukkot
24. Beginning of the Islam calendar — Awwal Muharram.
25. In the United States, Native American Day honors the first Americans.
27. This is National Good Neighbor Day to remind people to understand each other.

CHAPTER 22

Geography Booklet

A new tool is available for both parents and teachers who wish to expand their children's world. A 15-page booklet, "Helping Your Child Learn Geography," includes an outline map of the United States and may be *ordered from*:

> Consumer Information Center
> Dept. 466W
> Pueblo, CO 81009

Computer Software for Teaching Geography

"The Oregon Trail"
Provides students with an opportunity to cross America in the nineteenth century. Students practice decision-making and problem-solving skills as they learn about this important period in American History.

Order from:

> National School Products
> 101 East Broadway
> Maryville, TN 37801
> Telephone: (800) 627-9393

"National Inspirer"
This United States geography game for intermediate students is designed to be used in a one-computer classroom. It teaches state statistics like geographic area, population density and elevation while helping develop critical thinking and group cooperation skills. *Order below*:

"Where in the USA is Carmen Sandiego?"
Provides students with a large map of the United States, a copy of Fodor's USA Travel Guide and facts about U.S. and state history, economy and culture as well as geography.

This game delights students and requires attention to detail and note taking.

Order this software and the "National Inspirer" *from*:

> EISI
> 225 Grant Road
> Los Altos, CA 94024
> Telephone: (800) 955-5570

CHAPTER 23

Field Trip Graph

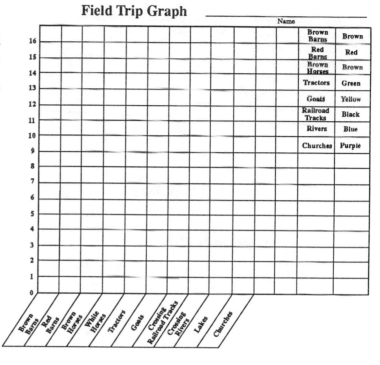

	Color
Brown Barns	Brown
Red Barns	Red
Brown Horses	Brown
Tractors	Green
Goats	Yellow
Railroad Tracks	Black
Rivers	Blue
Churches	Purple

For more detailed information on field trips, read chapter thirteen in <u>A First-Year Teacher's Guidebook for Success</u> by Bonnie Williamson.

Order from:

> Dynamic Teaching Company
> P.O. Box 276711
> Sacramento, CA 95827
> Telephone: (916) 351-1912

Teacher Resources

CHAPTER 24

Awesome Elementary School Physical Education Activities, pages 75-85
by Cliff Carnes
Order from:
   Dynamic Teaching Company
   P.O. Box 276711
   Sacramento, CA 95827
   Telephone: (916) 351-1912

CHAPTER 26

Tapes for Stress Reduction

"Understanding Stress and Learning to Relax"
by Dr. Paul Wood, M.D.
Order from:
   Dr. Paul Wood
   18800 Main Street, Suite 207
   Huntington Beach, CA 92648
   Telephone: (714) 842-0048

"Increased Relaxation with Relaxed Breathing"
by Dr. Reneau Peurifoy
Order from:
   LifeSkills Publications/Tapes
   P.O. Box 7915
   Citrus Heights, CA 95621
   Telephone: (916) 366-9444

"Wind in the Trees"
"Night in the Country"
"Caribbean Lagoon"
"English Meadow"
Order from:
   Syntonic Research, Inc.
   P.O. Box 18626
   Austin, TX 78760
   Telephone: (512) 459-4345

Books for Stress Reduction and Self-Improvement

The Relaxation and Stress Reduction Workbook
by Davis, Eshelan and McKay
Order from:
   New Harbinger Publications
   5674 Shattuck Avenue
   Oakland, CA 94609

Recreating Your Self
by Nancy J. Napier
Order from:
   W.W. Norton & Company, Inc.
   500 Fifth Avenue
   New York, NY 10110
   This book tells how to use affirmations.

Talk Sense To Yourself: The Language of Personal Power
by Chick Moorman
Order from:
   Personal Power Press
   P.O. Box 1130
   Bay City, MI 48706
   Telephone: (517) 686-3251